The Trade Winds

The Atlantic Slave Trade
- From Africa's Gold Coast to Haiti -

A Novel by

Ed Schwartz

First Edition - 2019

OAK CREEK *media*
Bluffton, Indiana

First Editor Copyright – 2019
by Ed Schwartz

ISBN: 978-1-7336505-0-2

Prologue

Historical fiction is a unique genre driven by facts. The people portrayed in *The Trade Winds* are created to fit history. Literary license is utilized to fill gaps without altering historical facts. Efforts are taken to accurately portray time-periods, locations and data. The locations and the roles they played in the Atlantic Slave Trade are real.

For instance, as you read this book, set in the late 18th century, you'll learn of the African Fante tribe who've resided in Ghana (formerly Slave-Coast Guinea) for hundreds of years and are still residing there today. Their exploited villages supplied thousands of slaves to the New World for centuries.

Today, Kakum National Park lies in the deep south of Ghana. It has 145 square miles of lush jungle teeming with forest elephants, bongo antelope, Diana monkeys, butterflies and birds. *The Trade Winds* begins in that part of Guinea's Fante-land in 1777.

The massive white Cape Coast Castle on the Atlantic African shoreline was built in the mid-17th century. It was used as a fort for defending the Gold Coast and later used exclusively in the Atlantic Slave Trade. Trafficked Africans were held captive there, in dungeons, awaiting transport via English and European ships to North, Central and South America as well as the Caribbean.

The plantations on the plains of Les Cayes in southwest Hispaniola (which today is Haiti) were very real. Today their countless ruins provide evidence of their vastness and place in history.

The graphic depictions of torture and discipline of African slaves in Saint-Domingue are derived from historical records. Tragically, what is depicted in *The Trade Winds* is supported by historical data.

In the 18th century, the Island of Hispaniola was divided into two parts – Spanish Santo Domingo to the east and French Saint-Domingue to the west. The eastern part today is the Dominican Republic and the western third is the country of Haiti.

The French domination of what is now Haiti was well documented. The massive wealth and volume of products leaving its Caribbean shores for Europe were not exaggerated. The inhumane treatment of the African slaves is likewise well documented and a part of history which mankind would like to erase. Lest we forget, the inhumane treatment of African slaves in North America mirrored what happened in French Saint-Domingue.

The Trade Winds seeks to portray, with as much accuracy as possible, the exploitation, trafficking and exodus of millions of African people from their homelands. It attempts to depict the horror, terror and tragedy which befell them in the New World.

Unfortunately, it's impossible to accurately reflect the excruciating pain, suffering, separation, loss, grief and fear which they endured for centuries... but we'll try.

This novel seeks to highlight the typical tragedies of the estimated twelve million Africans who were taken from their homeland and transported to the New World between 1525 and 1850. The reality of the masses is made personal by following just a few fictional Africans in their journey beginning in 1777.

Understanding history as well as present day reality sets the tone for how to change the status quo. The beautiful people of Haiti deserve a chance for a bright and successful future.

The title of this book, *The Trade Winds,* is based on the winds which pushed ships west from Africa to the Caribbean islands. Some theologians in the 17th and 18th century believed the winds were gifts and signs from God that slavery was blessed by Him. With that distorted theology, countless slaver ships made the treacherous journey with millions of Africans to the New World. They couldn't have done it without *The Trade Winds*.

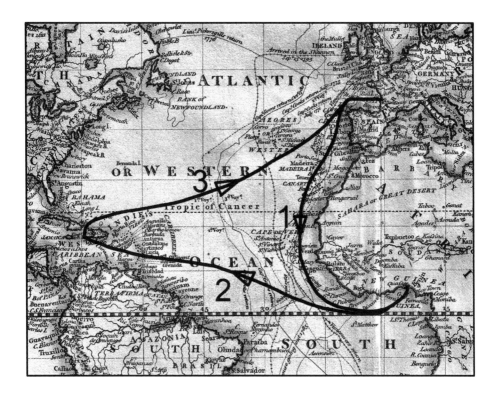

ATLANTIC TRADE TRIANGLE

The European and English slave ships sailed the three legs of the Atlantic Trade Triangle for centuries. Beginning in their home harbors, they sailed to various ports along the Atlantic seaboard of western Africa. There they sold or traded European cargo for African slaves.

The second leg took them to various ports in the America's and Caribbean where they sold the Africans and picked up local products.

The third leg of their voyage took them home to Europe and England where the many foreign products were sold.

The profits realized from each of the legs empowered an enormous and thriving business empire for Europe and England. Of course, each foreign location utilizing the Africans as slave labor, reaped their own gigantic profits.

The Trade Winds historical novel chronicles the various legs of the African Slave Trade making up the Atlantic Trade Triangle.

Chapter 1

April 10, 1777 – South Guinea (now Ghana) – Fante Tribe

ATU crouched quietly, immersed and invisible in the soft and wet ferns. The predictable sun had barely begun its slow journey into the brightening eastern sky. He carefully listened and watched. His body remained motionless though his eyes moved right and left. Periodically, he carefully swiveled his head to a new listening position. His lean and muscular fifteen-year-old body was poised but tense. His father had once told him to observe and mimic the deadly vipers who were always ready to strike. He'd learned his lessons well.

Just a few minutes earlier, the noisy Diana monkeys had been making a commotion above him when he entered his jungle hiding place, but they'd moved on.

Atu enjoyed these hunting forays into the damp rain forest. He didn't have much to compare his forest home to, as he didn't often venture far from it. Two years earlier he'd journeyed with his father and uncles northward to the flat plains. He'd been amazed to see mile after endless mile of dry and barren land. Though he'd been anxious to satisfy his youthful curiosity about what lay beyond his rain forest home, he'd decided one trip to the barren savannah would be enough.

On that earlier journey to the northern plain, he'd noticed scrub brush and stunted trees dotting the landscape. Some of the trees were home to large vultures which he knew were always an indication of death. They were waiting for the weak and solitary travelers.

But here, in his forest, the trees seemed to be filled with life. There were mahogany and other hardwood trees in the jungle and this particular area was known for trees that were always green. Rain and dew were generous in their creation of a beautiful, emerald green environment. The canopies of the trees stretched high above the ground and were so thick it was difficult to see the blue sky above.

The Diana monkeys normally living in the canopies were a staple of his tribe's diet. Though only the size of a dog, they were a delicacy for his family. His bow and arrow had brought many primates to his family's wooden platters.

The wart hogs and piglets, squealing and weaving their way through the ferns in the dense undergrowth were added to their village cooking pots when found.

The countless frogs and toads inhabiting the wet creeks and undergrowth assured Atu of a healthy population of snakes. Those of his tribe were always wary of the ever present vipers and cobras. He'd witnessed the violent deaths of several tribesmen who hadn't been careful enough. It was always a great day when those venomous predators could be killed and eaten. Though Atu was always barefoot, he instinctively knew in advance where his next steps would take him.

But, on this day, his quarry was something much larger and more desirable than wart hogs, monkeys or snakes. In this forest lived an animal which could feed him, his parents, two brothers, two sisters, as well as others in the tribe. It was the western lowland bongo. The bongo was one of the largest antelopes found in all of Africa. Atu had seen smaller antelopes of a different color on the plain, but they didn't compare to the forest bongo which could weigh up to 900 pounds.

Atu contemplated how fortunate he was at fifteen to be involved in this hunt, for it was the first time he was participating as a hunter. Always before he'd been one of the chasers along with other young boys. Though he couldn't see the other hunters, he knew where they were, camouflaged by ferns, likewise ready for what was to come.

It was then, in the distance he heard the clacking of wood against wood. He knew the chasers had begun their work!

He listened to the chasers drawing closer. He heard the sound of something coming his way! The breaking of branches, parting of vegetation and the pounding of hooves indicated something of significant size was approaching. Too far away for his spear, he got a fleeting glimpse of a bongo with its chestnut coat and the characteristic vertical white stripes disappearing into the thick forest.

Then, just as suddenly, there was another bongo much closer! Immediately, instinct brought him to his feet with his eight foot spear already swinging backward for the throw. The butt of the spear touched the ground behind him and simultaneously began its forward arc, until the timing was perfect and the spear pierced the air. The twenty foot distance was covered in an instant and found its mark directly behind the nearest front leg. The bongo leaped into the air, continued its momentum forward and crashed to the ground with a punctured heart.

Atu rushed to the side of the dying bongo. He watched the helpless, darting eyes as the blood and life ebbed out of the magnificent animal. Elated, he knew two things. First, there was a guarantee of meat for the cooking pots. Secondly, killing a bongo on his first trip as a hunter would seal his status within the tribe. Today, he'd become a man. He smiled.

Soon, his father Ekow and others joined him by the bongo. Atu clearly saw the pride in his father's eyes, but also knew it wasn't in his nature to openly affirm his eldest son. Instead, his father drew his knife and began removing the heavy spiral horns from the prize. He tied the horns together with a strip of leather and proudly hung them around his son's neck. Everyone knew the horns would be the sign of who the successful hunter had been.

The men quickly skinned, gutted and pieced out the large male bongo. They were soon joined by another group of men who would carry the meat, skin and offal of his prize. Atu noticed the admiring glances from the men as they saw the horns around his neck.

As the twenty or so men began their journey back to their home deeper in the rain forest, they began chanting and singing. The words were a victory song from ages past. Atu had heard this song from his youth and the words came instinctively as if they were part of the genes in his Fante body and mind. They were meant as a song of thanksgiving to their ancestors who were interceding with god on their behalf.

The twenty minutes it took to get back to the tribe's village permitted Atu ample time to reflect on his young life. Today's hunting success was no accident. He'd been prepared for years for this moment. From a small boy, he'd been taught the secrets of their forest.

His father had taught him how to track, as well as how to identify each track he noticed in the damp and rich earth. He'd learned the names and habits of each snake in their jungle. He knew which waterways had crocodiles and which toads were poisonous. He was taught where to find the food, roots and medicines which would keep their tribe alive and well.

He'd spent countless hours practicing with his bow and arrow as well as the steel tipped spear. He learned how to remain quietly in one spot without moving, barely breathing and waiting for food to come to him.

Again, he knew today's victory was not an accident. Fate had been kind to him today and he smiled as he thought of his future. When a Fante youth reached puberty, it was expected he'd soon marry. His father would now be busy in arranging a marriage for his eldest son. Today's kill would give his father bargaining leverage in finding a beautiful and talented bride for him.

Atu of course had been watching the young girls in their tribe. There were many rules to follow as to whom could marry whom, so the negotiations for marriage would be strictly adhered to. In any case, Atu was looking forward to marriage and beginning his new life as a husband, father and potential future leader of their Fante tribe.

He smelled the smoke of his village before arriving. It's pungent and rich wood smell indicated the cooking fires were lit. The women of the village had great confidence in the hunting abilities of their men and were ready. Then he began hearing the sounds of his village. Children emerged from the jungle and were running in front of the lead men who were carrying the meat. They likewise joined in the singing.

As they entered the village, Atu noticed all eyes were on him. His mother shyly lowered her head as he walked past her. He saw her pride but knew she was giving him honor by bowing her head to a new tribal hunter.

Young boys reached out and touched him and the bongo horns. He had become a man. He felt it. He basked in it. He was filled with elation and joy.

It was then he noticed her watching him.

Chapter 2

April 10, 1777 – South Guinea – Fante Tribe

FANTE villages consisted of multiple families living in a clearing large enough to accommodate huts and gardens. The communal environment created a closeness one could only call 'family'.

The families were 'one' and obviously cared for one another. One family's children blended into the children of other families. Parents in one family wouldn't hesitate to discipline or care for another parent's child. If a parent died, the rest of the village quickly filled the empty hole. Game, successfully hunted, belonged to the village, not to the successful hunter or his family. If someone had ill fortune, the village came alongside and helped. No one suffered alone.

When it was time to mill grain, the women of the village accomplished it as a group. When clothing was washed at the riverbank, they did it together.

One of the reasons to remain as a group was creating a defense mechanism. There were leopards which naturally preyed on the weak and defenseless, whether animal or human. The village was structured so no one lived apart from others. They were connected in play, work, hunting and worship of their god and ancestors.

The village had a perimeter fence of brush, thorns and branches which were intertwined to keep dangers out and create security.

The homes were made of dried mud with branches and twigs inserted for stability. The huts were comfortable, large and tall so a man could stand upright. The arched doorways and windows could be closed at night with wooden shutters. The exterior walls were decorated with bright colored designs made from root dyes.

It was a peaceful place to live. The center of the village had a communal cooking area. Multiple fires with several pots were maintained throughout the day. Cooking began early in the morning to assure a large mid-day meal.

Now, the cooking area was busy. Several young girls were cutting vegetables, roots and plants for three of the water-filled pots. Young children were running and playing among the huts. Two of the young teenaged girls were talking together as they stirred the vegetables over the open fire.

Efi said, "My mother told me last night that men south of here were cutting down trees. They'll sell them to men on large boats at the shore."

Kisi responded, "My father told me the same thing yesterday. He was concerned because having strangers that close to us could be a danger."

The girls were fifteen-years-old and had been close friends for as long as they could remember. They'd learned the village and ancestral ways early in life. Cooking, caring for the family, gardening, and laundry had become a way of life for them. Instinctively they knew what lay before them each day and dutifully they did what was necessary to maintain a consistent and predictable life. They'd learned predictability wasn't boring, it was security and safety.

Neither Efi nor Kisi had ever been to the ocean which was twenty miles to the south. In fact, neither of the girls had ever been more than a mile from their village. All their village needed to survive was nearby and there was simply no reason to venture further. Though some of the men had traveled further to trade their food for weapons or other necessities, the women stayed safely in the village.

Kisi continued, "My father talked to a man who'd been to the coast once. He said you couldn't see land on the other side. He spoke about the large boats he saw on the water and said he was glad to get back to his village."

Efi said, "I wonder sometimes what life is like outside of our village, but I think it's better to stay here and be safe."

Kisi agreed, "Yes, I think you're right. Mother told me last week that..."

Suddenly, both girls turned to identify the commotion erupting on the west side of the village. They heard children singing and yelling. Then they saw the men of the village returning from their hunt. The first ones were carrying meat on their shoulders. Two more had a bongo hide rolled together and resting on their heads.

Then, emerging from the jungle they saw a young man with antelope horns around his neck. They both recognized Atu at the same time. As he walked into the village he was welcomed by the tribal villagers as a hero. His eyes connected with the dark black eyes of the beautiful and young Fante woman, Kisi.

Chapter 3

RENARD held his ceramic tankard of ale tightly, closed his eyes and relaxed. Then someone asked, "Are you sleeping, my friend?"

He opened one eye to see his shipmate Lucien. "I'm not sleeping now, am I? Thanks for robbing me of my well-deserved rest."

Lucien said, "Aye, a well-deserved rest. I know what you mean. That was a long eight months at sea. It was surely that!"

"Do you have a point to make Lucien, or are you simply a devil in disguise seeking to rob me of my drink and rest?"

"I may be a devil, but I know I'm sitting next to one too. You've taught me well."

They'd been shipmates on an eight month voyage to Africa and the America's. Just the day before, they had returned to Bordeaux.

Lucien asked, "So, when do you intend to ship out again?"

Renard responded, "I think after I've drunk fifty kegs of ale, sipped a barrel full of whiskey, and slept solid for a hundred nights."

"There's no doubt in my mind you'll accomplish all of that and then some. How are you going to pay for all of that whiskey and ale?"

Renard held tightly to his tankard handle and with his other hand patted his flintlock pistol and large knife in his leather waist-belt. "I think there are many coins in businessmen's pockets that would be much happier in my money bag. I just need to find the coins and remove them from their owners."

"Might be I'll see you around again, Renard. Don't get drunk and fall off the docks."

Renard playfully hit him on his shoulder as Lucien rose to leave the table.

He finished the tankard and yelled to the barkeeper to bring a bottle of whiskey. Renard was enjoying the buzz from the ale and knew this would be a night to remember, or likely forget. He smiled to himself.

He watched the barkeeper retrieve a bottle from under the counter and deftly remove the cork. He never ceased to be amazed at this particular barman who only had one arm. The other arm had been removed below the elbow and the stump had been fitted with a protruding steel hook.

"So, barkeep, how'd you lose that arm? Did you get in the way of your girlfriend's knife?"

Raising his hook toward the rough-hewn ceiling, he replied, "Ah, if you weren't a paying customer, I'd poke you in the eye with my hook!

"It was in 1758 on a sailing vessel to Boston that I lost my arm. A storm was brewing to the nor'east and the first mate told me to loose a sail on the mizzenmast. At the top, I slipped and fell. I had tied a rope around my arm for safety and was hanging from the top-yard by that arm way too long before someone climbed up to retrieve me. The arm was broken and a bone were sticking through the skin. The ship's doctor cut off my arm. I thought hanging from the mizzenmast was horrible, but that was nothing compared to the pain when he started sawing. The only good thing about losing my arm is I didn't have to work the rest of the voyage and I got a daily dose of whiskey for the pain. It was almost like a holiday."

Renard was tough and there was little that scared him, but imagining a doctor cutting off his arm made him cringe.

The barkeeper saw the grimace and said, "You mean a rough old saltwater crab like you can't handle the thought of a little pain?"

"I'll have to give you credit, barkeep. You've been through some tough things I'll likely not experience and I'm surely hopeful I never do!"

The barkeeper went back to his liquor selling business and Renard got back to his drinking.

Much later, Renard lurched to the door and went outside into the midnight air. He smelled the dirty Garonne River. He started staggering toward the dock but decided against it as he remembered Lucien's caution about falling into the river. So, clumsily, he sat in the dark alley and leaned against the tavern's wall. He held his bottle tightly and took another swig. Then he passed out.

His body began swaying side to side and Renard thought he was once again aboard his ship on a rough ocean. He opened his eyes to see four men grasping his arms and legs and carrying him away from the tavern. He tried to yell, but his mouth was gagged with a rag. He fought desperately until the men accidentally dropped him. He tried to stand but his arms and legs were tied. They picked him up and roughly carried him up the cobblestone street to another dock. As they headed up the gangplank of a three-masted freighter, Renard saw the name of the ship, *L'ange D'or* or *The Golden Angel*.

The men took him below deck and tied him to a large forged steel ring embedded in a rough-hewn wooden post. A single candle barely lit the area. Renard saw three other men shackled to other posts. The four captors retreated to the top deck.

Renard was able to spit out the gag. He looked at his belt and saw his flintlock and knife were gone, but he was almost sadder to know he'd lost his bottle of whiskey. One of the other men said, "Welcome laddie boy to *The L'ange D'or*. You've been shanghaied and it appears we'll be shipmates."

"When's this ship sailing and where's it going?"

"We're not sure, but rumor has it that in two days we'll be leaving Bordeaux and heading to the Gold Coast of Africa."

Renard cursed at his carelessness. He'd certainly done his share of abducting other men to fill a crews roster, but this was his first shanghai. He'd just gotten off a ship and now was shipping out again.

Chapter 4

ANTOINETTE was devastated. Depressed, she sat in one of the two chairs she owned and wept. Her small cottage was cluttered and unkempt. She was reliving what had happened just two weeks earlier.

She and her son Pierre had gone to the Bordeaux dock on the Garonne River to welcome their husband and father home from his six month sailing voyage on the L'ange D'or. With smiles on their faces they watched the crew disembark and meet their sweethearts or families. Finally, Captain Jean Moise descended to the dock and stretched a rope across the gangplank walkway indicating he was the last one leaving the ship. Their smiles now gone, they waited and watched, but no one else appeared.

Antoinette and Pierre approached the captain and she said, "My husband Bernard was on your ship and we've not seen him. Where is he?"

Captain Jean hesitated, but then said, "I regret bringing you the news of your husband's death aboard my ship. A day after boarding our ship here in Bordeaux, we entered the Bay of Biscay. A squall came up abruptly at midnight. Your husband was on watch and was somehow swept into the bay by the wind. It was a freak thing and a terrible misfortune. I'm so sorry for the loss to you and your son."

That news had been bad enough, but it got worse. Her husband had been on contract with the captain and would've brought home the much needed money for their debts. Now, there'd be no money since his life was taken early in the voyage.

Antoinette said to the captain, "I have no money. My husband was bringing the funds we needed to pay our debts and loans. How can we survive without money?"

"I'm truly sorry. Your husband had only given me one day of labor instead of the six months he contracted for. I have nothing to give you."

"I'll lose my house. My son won't be able to finish his education. I do laundry for others, but that's only enough to buy the food we need. What can I do?"

Captain Jean stroked his heavy grey beard and paused. Then he said, "I can loan you the money, if you give me collateral. What can you provide?"

"I only have a small cottage that I still don't own. I have nothing else."

Again in thought, the captain said, "I have an idea. If it's all right with you, we'll talk in your house privately. May I walk you to your home?"

Arriving, the captain then explained his plan to Antoinette, "I'm sorry for your situation. It's sad indeed, but you're not the first to lose a husband on a sailing trip. Each time it's difficult for me to share such sad news."

He paused and then said, "Your son would be of great value to me on my next sailing trip in two weeks. I'm in need of someone for my personal assistance as a cabin boy. If you permit me to take him for six months, I'll consider the loan paid in full."

With a gasp, Antoinette realized she had no choice. Her only son was soon to be an indentured servant.

~

Two weeks had seemed like an eternity, yet there had been a lot to do. Her fifteen-year-old son Pierre had been devastated when he'd heard of his father's death. He felt worse when his mother told him his formal education was over, his dreams of becoming a carpenter's apprentice were dashed, and he was going to sea.

Incredulous, he said, "Mama, what have you done? I'm only fifteen! I don't know anything about the sea. It just took my father and now it's taking me?"

She'd wept with him. Holding him, she said, "Pierre, there's nothing else to do. If you don't do this, we lose our home and we'll both live on the streets. This way we'll both have a place to live when you come home in six months."

"I'm terrified Mama. I hear stories about the lives of sailors. I know nothing other than living in Bordeaux with you. I'm just a school boy and I don't think I'll survive."

Antoinette held him again and they both wept. This was the day he was to leave.

~

Pierre carried his small carpet bag of clothing and walked slowly with his mother to the Garonne River docks. They stopped in front of the large ship with the name *L'ange D'or* on its bow.

They both stared at Pierre's future. The three masted cargo ship was one hundred feet long and twenty-five feet wide.

Antoinette with a smile said, "The name of this ship is *Golden Angel*. I think that's a good omen of safe passage for you."

Pierre grimaced. "Mama, how can you say that? Do you think it gives me comfort? That's the same ship Papa was on when he was killed! I don't think there were any golden angels protecting him."

Captain Jean was standing on the deck talking to a sailor. Looking down, he noticed his new cabin boy and Antoinette. He quickly made his way down the gangplank to the dock and shook Antoinette's hand and put his large, calloused hand on Pierre's shoulder.

"Welcome Pierre."

Pierre hung his head and said nothing.

"I'm sure this is a difficult time for both of you. But, Madame, I want you to know I'll do all I can to keep your son safe and return him to you in six months. I think he'll learn a lot about life and the world in these next months at sea. We'll consider this journey an education for him. We'll be sailing in a couple of days but I'll need this time to get him ready for our departure."

Neither mama nor Pierre had anything to say. Antoinette gave her son a hug and a long kiss on his forehead.

Pierre followed the captain up the gangplank. He stopped at the top-deck and looked down at his mother. He could see the tears streaming down her face. She looked tiny and vulnerable as she waved goodbye to her only son. She knew more than most about the dangers on the open seas and the strange ports. She discerned her son would leave as a boy and return as a man. She also knew Pierre would never be the same, nor would she.

Pierre waved and wiped the tears from his eyes. Captain Jean said, "Pierre, for you to survive these next six months, those will need to be the last tears anyone sees. There are forty-two men on this ship. Some of them are the roughest and toughest men in French society. In fact, most are outcasts to the point they're not in anyone's society. They live for only one thing. Themselves. They cut no mercy for others. They'll not give you anything, but they'll take everything. I'm almost a stranger to you, but I may be the only one you can trust on this voyage. I'll do my best to keep my promise to your mother in trying to keep you safe."

He continued, "As I said, there are forty-two men on board. Myself as captain, a first-mate who's my right-hand man, the second and third mates, a surgeon and three cabin boys, one of them being yourself. The other thirty-four men do all the manual work on board. Come. Let me show you your berth and we'll look around the ship."

They started at the rear or stern of the ship on the main-deck and descended a small and narrow staircase to the captain's quarters. Pierre saw a table with six chairs, books, brass instruments on a shelf, several swords hanging on the wall as well as flintlock guns. The captain said, "These are my quarters. No one enters unless I give them permission. The officers will eat here with me and you'll be our server. You're permitted to come and go, but only if you ask permission from me first."

Exiting through the door into a small passageway, Pierre saw a small bed inset into a wall. The captain said, "This is your sleeping berth. The other two cabin boys will be in the forecastle with the crewmen. Due to the promise I gave your mother, I'll keep you close and you'll serve me personally."

Returning to the top deck, the captain pointed out the helm above the captain's quarters. There was a large wooden ship's wheel and the bittacle which housed the compass.

Leaning over the stern he pointed to the submerged rudder which steered the ship. They walked mid-ship and the captain pointed out the usages of each of the three masts. Walking to the forward part of the ship or bow he pointed to the long bowsprit beam angling out over the water which controlled some of the foremast sails. It'd lead them to whatever lay ahead.

Many of the men were busy working on the main deck coiling ropes and stowing gear. Some were busy swabbing the deck. Others were patching and sewing sails. A few were oiling and working on the deck cannons. Most gave only a moment's glance at Pierre.

Taking the small stairs below the forecastle, they entered the crew's quarters. Another stairway led them further below. As they entered the next deck, it was packed with many wooden barrels and wooden crates.

The captain explained, "We've loaded the ship full of products which we'll trade at the Gold Coast in Guinea, Africa. We'll be unloading at the Cape Coast port in about twenty-five days. There we'll be loading Africans to carry to the Caribbean island called Hispaniola. The barrels contain liquor and the crates are full of beads, knives, guns, clothing and other items the African tribes want. These are items we'll be using to trade with the Africans before we sail to Hispaniola."

There were four decks total, including the top-side main deck. The three lower decks were full of more barrels and crates. When they arrived at the bottom deck, Pierre noticed four men chained to the wooden beams supporting the upper decks. He asked, "Who are those men?"

"Yes, that deserves an explanation. As captain of the ship, it's my responsibility to make sure the owners of the ship are well-served. They expect me to get products and materials to a particular place at specific times. To accomplish that I must maintain schedules. It takes a certain amount of crewmen to make it happen. When I get close to sailing time, if I don't have enough crew, I need to do things I don't like to fulfill my obligations. I was in need of four additional men and couldn't find them. There are many ships leaving Bordeaux and the need for sailors is competitive. Sometimes I need to be creative in how to fill out my crew. These four men are experienced sailors, but each needed, shall we say, a little extra persuasion to join us. When we reach the high seas, they'll be released and become a valuable part of our crew."

Pierre looked at the men and realized they were just as much indentured servants as himself. He felt compassion for them and wondered if they'd begun their ocean careers years ago as some captain's cabin boy.

Chapter 5

April 11, 1777 – South Guinea, Africa

DARIFA was dreaming about lush meadows filled with beautiful flowers when she was jolted awoke by someone lying beside her. She spontaneously cried out in surprise only to be kicked.

The woman next to her whispered, "Be quiet or they'll beat you!"

Darifa sadly replied, "I'm sorry. I was dreaming. When I was in my home I'd sometimes have nightmares and wake up in a peaceful hut. Now I have pleasant dreams and wake up in a nightmare."

She looked over the top of the woman lying beside her to see many small campfires burning in a clearing. As she listened in the darkness she heard the steady sound of breathing and various other snorts and snoring. She heard a child crying in the distance and then a muffled sound as she pictured a mother clamping her child's mouth shut for fear of reprisal.

Her neck was incredibly sore from the never-ending rub of the rough, wooden shackle. In fact, there was almost no part of her that didn't hurt. They'd been walking for days, and if her memory was correct, it'd been eleven days since she'd been abducted from her village in the north. As near as she could tell, nine men, women and children had been taken from her Fante village.

They'd joined a caravan of another one hundred and thirty other victims. Over the last eleven days, another forty-six were added from Guinea villages along the route to the southern coast.

Unable to sleep, Darifa started thinking about that fateful night eleven days earlier.

She'd been awakened by shouting during the middle of the night. Then her ankle was grabbed by a huge African man who pulled her through the dirt to the scrub brush surrounding her village. As she was pulled through an opening in the security fence made of brush and thorns, she felt her flesh tear. She screamed and heard the screams of others. She knew she wasn't alone in her unfolding tragedy and agony.

She never saw what happened to her husband and six-year-old daughter. She feared for their lives as she saw their hut erupting in flames. She had screamed again. Then a large fist had smashed her in the face and everything went black.

She had no idea how long she was unconscious, but when she awoke, she realized her neck was secured in some kind of wooden yoke.

The sounds of crying, periodic screaming, men yelling and children sobbing created a new kind of hell for Darifa. In fear and apprehension, she waited.

At first dawn she tried to get a look at the apparatus around her neck. The five foot tree branch had a V on one end, which nearly encircled her neck. There was a steel rod and pin locking it. The yoke's long wooden shank extended behind her. She saw many men and women with the same wooden shackles. The children had ropes around their necks which were tied to other children.

An African man forced the women to line up in groups of six. Darifa had been the second one in a line. The man grabbed the long wooden shank of the first woman and placed it on Darifa's shoulder and forced her hand to hold it tight. Then the woman behind her held Darifa's shank. The rest did the same. The six women stood in the early morning sunshine until they were forced to begin walking.

The scene was impossible for Darifa to comprehend. She watched as many groups of men, women and children began walking south.

She looked at her captors. She didn't recognize their language. They were African but obviously from different tribes than her own. It only took two of them to manage five or six groups of captives.

If someone in a group became exhausted or began walking slowly, they were beaten with a whip. If it happened again, the entire group *was beaten. If it happened a third time, the weak person was released from their yoke, killed and left for the animals.*

Darifa's mind drifted from her recollections of the recent past and into the present. Tomorrow would be day twelve. She'd no idea how many more days they'd be walking through the jungle on their way south. Then Darifa fell asleep.

Chapter 6

April 12, 1777 – South Guinea – Fante Village

FANTE tribesmen were gathered in the center of the village. Everyone could smell the cooking bongo antelope meat and vegetables in the simmering communal pots. There was no need to beat the drums to summon the villagers to the noon feast, as the smells had done a better job than the drums could ever have done.

Atu and his mother were sitting on a log at the side of the clearing waiting for the feast to begin. She was clearly proud to be with her son, the new hunter. The drums were beating. Sweat was building on the faces and bodies of the drummers maintaining the rhythmic sounds of their ancestors. The wooden hollow drums were covered by a pulsating animal hide stretched over one end of a log. Tribal dancing was always the end result of the incessant drums.

Soon, young women began a slow entrance into the village clearing. Almost as one, they swayed and stepped together to the drums heartbeat. Young men entered the clearing. Standing opposite from the girls they began their own rhythm and dance. Atu watched as the group became larger and larger. Watching them was almost like watching a large cobra move through the ferns of his beloved jungle. Each of the young men and women were simply one part of something much larger than themselves.

It seemed to Atu that everything which transpired in their village was about family. They were all part of something larger than themselves and each made the whole better. Everyone was needed and everyone had purpose.

It was then Atu saw his father Ekow enter the clearing with another man. His heart nearly stopped as he recognized Kwaku, another tribal elder. Atu's successful hunting trip yesterday, his quick elevation to that of a hunter and his emergence into the tribe as a man happened quickly. Atu mentally thanked his ancestors for interceding with the good father-god for delivering the bongo to his hiding place.

The clearing became quiet. The drums and dancing stopped. All eyes were upon the two tribal elders in the center. The two men grabbed one another's arms and touched their cheeks together.

Atu knew what it meant. Both men had something in common. Each had a child ready for marriage and the arrangement for Atu to marry the other man's daughter was sealed.

Atu was shocked. He looked around the clearing at the many people. It was then he saw Kwaku's daughter Kisi standing with her head bowed and looking very beautiful. Atu stood and walked to his father. Kisi walked to her father. The drummers began their rhythmic beating.

Awkwardly, Atu and Kisi stood at the center of attention in the middle of their Fante village in southern Guinea. The world seemed to stop. When Atu looked into Kisi's eyes he knew she was just as pleased as he was.

The tribal elders sat together. The cooks brought them a generous helping of Atu's bongo, vegetables and fruit. Atu's father invited Atu and Kisi to join them. Atu was feeling very uncomfortable. He thought he'd rather be facing a 900 pound bongo plummeting directly toward him than to be in the middle of all these people with Kisi. Then again, as he focused on Kisi, he knew he was exactly where he needed to be, and more importantly, where he wanted to be. His pounding heart told him that he was in love.

When everyone had eaten, his father stood and announced, "The betrothal will be for seven days. Then my son Atu and Kwaku's daughter Kisi will be married. That length of time will be needed for the passing of gifts between our families, as well as preparing for the wedding feast."

Again, Atu looked at Kisi and sensed the love she had for him. He was looking forward to spending time with her and learning more about her. It was difficult to believe she'd be his wife in seven days! He'd known her all her life but tribal tradition taught the young men and women to keep emotions to themselves until they were ready for marriage. Yesterday on his entrance into the village with the bongo horns around his neck was a non-verbal announcement that he was a man and ready for a wife.

Chapter 7

April 14, 1777 – Bordeaux, France – Garonne River Docks

PIERRE couldn't believe how quickly the last three days had gone by. His mother had come to the dock each day for a hopeful glimpse of him. Each day he was able to wave to her. She'd smile and then walk back to their home. He knew, without a doubt, of her love for him. He was finally reconciling himself to becoming the man in his family.

From dawn to dusk he was given work on board the ship. He'd never worked so hard. The other cabin boys were two years older than he was and at seventeen, they'd already been to Africa twice. They seemed hardened. He hoped he wouldn't become what he perceived these boys to be.

One of his many duties on board was to bring food to the four men in the bottom hold. They were dirty from their days of being chained to the beams. Twice a day he gave them a bucket to use as their toilet. Then he had to dump it over the side of the ship into the Garonne River. Pierre had never been around such vulgar characters before. The cursing exploding from their mouths shocked him. They teased him with stories and questions which made him extremely uncomfortable. No one would ever accuse him of being slow if they watched how quickly he could take care of these men. Their laughter haunted him and he couldn't get away quickly enough.

Returning to the main deck, Pierre was surprised to see the crewmen readying the sails. The captain was at the helm giving orders to the mates. The first mate was passing those orders on to the second and third mate who passed them on to the crew. Pierre was amazed at how efficient the crew was in preparing the ship for their voyage.

He scanned the docks for any sign of his mother. She was nowhere to be found. It was still early morning and he realized she'd likely miss their departure. He was glad to have seen her the day before.

The ropes tying the *L'ange D'or* to the dock were loosened, retrieved and coiled neatly along the gunwale. The captain called for the mainsail to drop. A breeze filled the sail and the ship moved into the Garonne River. At the wheel, the captain skillfully steered the ship to midstream and began the northwest fifteen mile trip to merge with the River Dordogne. Then it was another forty mile jaunt to the Bay of Biscay. The captain wanted to make the bay before dusk.

Pierre was enjoying the cruise and was amazed at the number of factories along the river. Along the shoreline, he could see young children waving at the ship. He waved back with a smile.

Finally reaching the end of the Dordogne, he walked to the forecastle to get a view of the upcoming Bay of Biscay. He'd never been to the ocean before and was immediately spellbound with the wide expanse of water before him. The bowsprit pointed the ship forward. He wondered what was ahead.

The captain had said the voyage to Africa could take about twenty-five days. Suddenly, he heard the captain's voice booming from the helm at the stern of the ship. "Pierre, I need you!

"Go with the third mate and release the four men in the hold. It's time to get them to work. When you bring them to the top deck, get them buckets of water to wash themselves. Then go below and clean up the hold where they were."

Pierre followed the mate below-deck. He knew the four men were no novice seamen. They knew exactly what would happen and when.

The shanghaied or kidnapped sailor named Renard held up his hands to the mate. A key was inserted and Renard slowly stood. His legs seemed a bit wobbly, so he shook them out and waited for the other three men to be released. Pierre led the men to the top-deck.

Giving them their buckets of water, Pierre stood back as they washed the filth from their bodies and took in the warm sunshine. The captain told Pierre to get them clean clothing from the second deck.

The men quickly dressed and stood waiting for instructions. Once given, there were no questions. These were able-bodied seamen who knew their way around ships.

Renard looked at Pierre, smiled and winked. Pierre was so surprised, he reacted physically with a jerk. He had no idea what the smile and wink meant.

After dusk, Pierre served dinner to the captain, two of the three mates and the surgeon. After the meal each of the men had a snifter of brandy. It seemed the journey wouldn't be short on alcohol. Pierre now knew what the barrels held.

After the others left, the captain said, "Pierre, you seem to have accepted your fate on board the ship. I want to say that I think you'll be a fine cabin boy."

"Thank you captain."

The captain said, "I noticed one of the four men you brought from the hold seemed to give you a special message with his smile and wink."

"Yes sir, I saw it too."

"Can I give you some advice?"

"Yes sir. This is all new to me."

The captain seemed cautious in how he continued, "Some men are not like most men. I think perhaps this Renald is someone to be careful of. None of these men are what your mother would call good men, but Renald may be a danger to you. Don't take his smile and wink as a special friendship. You may find he has other motives. I'll make sure the mates are aware of my concern for you."

The worry on the captain's face caused Pierre to sense a fear within himself that wasn't easily relieved. He was thankful for the warning and decided to be careful, even more careful than he'd been.

The entry into the Bay put them on a westerly course until they turned southward and then westward to go around the Spanish and Portuguese coastline. Though they were a few miles offshore, Pierre could still see land which continued to give him a sense of security.

The captain hollered, "Pierre, come here."

Pierre joined the captain at the helm.

"Pierre, I think it's important for you to know we're at the spot where your father was lost in the squall. Maybe in some small way it'll help for you to know where your father is buried."

Pierre returned to the gunwale and looked at the Bay of Biscay. He wasn't sure what to feel, but seeing the spot where his father died seemed to help bring closure to one of the unknowns in his life.

As he crawled wearily into his bunk that night he blew out the animal-fat tallow candle. The rocking motion of the ship lulled him to sleep quickly.

Chapter 8

April 15, 1777 – South Guinea – Fante Tribe

KISI had been excited when she observed her father entering the village clearing with Atu's father and knew immediately what it meant. Tradition was being followed. She knew their fathers and mothers had discussed the dowry of marriage. All seemed to be in order and Kisi couldn't help smiling.

She'd known there was something special about Atu. He had a confidence and strength unusual for a fifteen-year-old. She'd been watching him for a year with a growing appreciation and respect. She also knew there were other young women her age watching Atu as well. There wasn't any room in the Fante tradition to permit interaction other than within a group. Before marriage, intimacy was forbidden among the tribe and strict rules governed male and female relationships.

It'd been three days since the bongo feast and the announcement of their betrothal. Today was a special day. With the blessing and trust of their parents, the two would spend the day together talking about the future.

A noise came from the front entrance of her family's mud hut. A clicking sound indicated Atu's arrival. Kisi's mother stood and went to the opening. She invited Atu inside. The conversation between Kisi and Atu began awkwardly.

"Good morning", Atu said clumsily.

Kisi stood with her head lowered and responded with, "Good morning. How was your night?"

"It was good. And you?"

"Yes, it was good."

Atu hesitantly looked at Kisi's mother and asked, "May I spend some time today talking with your daughter?"

Mawusi smiled broadly and said, "Yes. But be careful and bring her back before dark."

Relieved, Atu replied, "Yes. Yes I will. Thank you."

Kisi and Atu left the village and entered the jungle heading west.

Kisi smiled and asked, "Where are we going?"

Atu smiled with a large grin and said, "I have something very special to show you."

They continued to talk as they walked for twenty minutes. Then, Atu stopped beside the Kakum River. They sat on the bank and watched the water flowing.

He said, "Maybe if we dropped a coconut in the water, it'd find its way to the ocean."

Kisi laughed, "Should we make a small boat and see where it goes? Maybe it'll take us to the ocean to the south."

Atu laughed, "Ha, I've traveled outside of our beautiful jungle and I don't think there's a better place to be. I think we'll stay here."

"What do you think the ocean is like? I've heard there are fish large enough to swallow a man."

"I don't know about that. But I do know there's many fish in this river small enough for me to swallow and that's good enough for me."

Atu stood up and held out his hand to help her stand. "I have something else to show you."

They walked another five minutes to a huge tree. Near the bottom were branches permitting easy climbing. With Atu helping Kisi, they climbed to a large limb near the top. It overlooked the Kakum River and jungle. Sitting side by side, they were comfortable.

Kisi said, "This is beautiful. I've never been in this area before. It's very peaceful and quiet. I think you've sat in this spot before?"

"Many times I've sat here and dreamed about the future. Some of those dreams were about you."

He continued, "I'm hoping the river won't be peaceful and quiet today. This is an area where elephant herds come to drink and wallow in the mud. I've watched them many times. There are minerals in the ground here attracting them."

He laughed and said, "Can you imagine what the tribal leaders would've said if I'd have speared an elephant instead of a bongo! Maybe I'd have gotten ten wives!"

Kisi smiled at Atu's humor. She was content and happy.

Then she laughed and said, "I'm not sure what you'd have done with an elephant on the end of your spear, just as I'm not sure what you'd have done with ten wives."

"When I went to the northern plains with my father and uncles, we saw elephants which were larger than these forest elephants."

Kisi said, "You've traveled and seen so much. You seem to know a lot about many things. Are you sure you'll be content staying here in the jungle?"

"I've seen other places but nothing compares to this. Everything I need is here. The only thing I was missing was you. With you by my side, there's nothing more for me to see or have."

Kisi smiled.

Atu pointed to an elephant slowly walking along the river. He whispered to Kisi, "There's the bull. He's making sure this area is safe. When he's satisfied, you'll hear him rumble and see the females and the young following."

Over the next five minutes the bull, four females and two young calves made their way toward the large tree. They stopped and entered the water. It was breathtaking to be so close to such huge animals and watch them as a family.

They dug their long tusks into the vegetation and ate leaves and marsh grass. The water was rich in minerals and the mud was cool and relaxing. This family was enjoying itself immensely.

Atu whispered, "I think this elephant family is just like me. They have everything they need right here."

They watched for another hour as the elephants continued to feed, wallow and relax.

Then, the male lifted his head. His trunk extended into the air and his large ears stretched outward. He was detecting sounds and scent. Atu knew an elephant could sense sounds traveling through the ground and into their feet. With baby elephants in the herd, the bull would be very cautious. Possibly a leopard was in the area and interested in one of the young elephants.

Almost noiselessly, the herd began moving across the river into the jungle. Atu wondered what had startled them.

Atu helped Kisi climb down from the tree. At the bottom, they sat and leaned against the tree. While talking, a movement upstream caught Atu's eye. He saw two men drinking from the river. One of the men saw Atu at the same time.

The two men disappeared into the jungle. Kisi asked, "Who were they?"

"I don't know. I don't think they're Fante."

They continued to talk. Suddenly Atu heard a noise and stood. In the clearing on the other side of the tree, he saw five men, all armed with spears. They were large Africans and appeared threatening. Instinctively Kisi grabbed Atu's arm. Atu looked behind him to see the deep river and knew their retreat was blocked.

The men began speaking loudly in a language Atu didn't understand. They repeated it. Finally two of the men approached them and pointed their spears at them. Atu tensed but didn't respond as he had no weapon. The larger of the two brought up the butt of his spear and hit Atu on the side of his head. Atu fell. Kisi screamed. He dazedly stood up.

Immediately the two men tied their wrists. The five men began pushing Atu and Kisi into the jungle heading north. They were terrified.

After a five minute walk, they emerged into a clearing. Sitting in the undergrowth were groups of men, women and children. Atu could see fifty or sixty people.

The five men pushed Atu and his bride-to-be to the ground. She looked at the women around her. They were all her age and older with the oldest about the age of her own mother.

They were very dirty and Kisi saw fear in some of their eyes. In others she saw compassion. Some had eyes which showed no emotion. In all of the eyes she saw sadness.

Each of the Africans on the ground had a large wooden stick and yoke around their neck. Some were bleeding from the chafing. Most of the captives were naked. Kisi looked at their feet. She gasped when she saw their tattered feet with bleeding blisters and thorn-ripped flesh. She wondered how long these people had been walking.

Men came through the group with buckets of water. They went to each person and lingered long enough for each to take a handful or two. Other men were coming with fruit and vegetables which were given to each person.

Another man who was obviously a leader came into the clearing. A man walking beside him was carrying two yokes and walked to Kisi and Atu. He pushed the yoke around Atu's neck. There were holes in the end of the yoke through which he pushed a steel rod. He pushed a clasp into the rod end to secure it. The yoke was tight around Atu's throat and made it difficult to swallow.

Another man put a yoke around Kisi's neck and secured it. The helper grabbed the pole end of Atu's yoke and pulled him to his feet. He towed him into the jungle away from Kisi, but Atu looked back in time to see terror and tears on her face.

Atu was full of shame, fear and regret. He felt shame for not keeping Kisi safe. Fear about what might happen to them. Regret that he'd gone so far from their village and he'd told no one where they were going. What would their parents think when they didn't return at dusk?

He knew men from his village would look for them, but the jungle was large and changing every day and night. What were the chances anyone would find this spot? It was remote.

What did these people want? Who were they? Where were they going?

Chapter 9

April 15, 1777 – South Guinea

DARIFA had watched as five men led a young African man and woman into the clearing. They were clearly terrified and it brought back memories of other captives joining their procession over the last days. She knew she'd been just as terrified when she was kidnapped. She felt compassion for them and knew they had no idea of what was ahead.

They'd pushed the couple into the ferns beside her group of women. Then they proceeded with the ritual of putting on the neck yokes and pulling the young man into the jungle. Darifa saw the look of desperation on the young man's face as he looked into the eyes of the young woman. She knew there was a special bond between them. It was no different than what she'd felt with her husband and that brought tears to her eyes.

The guards left the young girl in the grass with her group. Someone spoke to the girl, but the girl had a confused look on her face as she responded. It was clear their languages hadn't been the same. But excitedly, Darifa recognized the new girl's Fante dialect.

It'd been fifteen days since Darifa had been captured. She'd counted 203 men, women and children in their group. She knew some of the large group had been walking for days before getting to her village. Now two more were added bringing the total to 205 sad victims who had been torn from their family, friends and villages.

Darifa and Kisi were in the same group on the jungle floor. Darifa whispered a 'Hello' in Fante to Kisi who turned quickly and smiled. Both knew it'd be impossible to carry on a conversation without reprisal, so they merely smiled.

~

Meanwhile, Atu had been drug to another clearing where many men were squatting or lying in the jungle undergrowth. The guards left him there and immediately Atu thought about running away. He knew it'd be difficult with a five foot branch tied to his neck but he was desperate. Then he saw the guards on the perimeter. They had spears. Some had a weapon which looked like a long wooden stick with a round iron piece sticking out the end. There were several guards and Atu's hopes of running quickly vanished.

Atu sat on the ground next to a man laying quietly. Looking at the man, Atu saw bloody wounds on his back from a whipping. The man was emaciated. Then he realized the man was dead! Atu recoiled from the death before him, and cautiously moved toward another group of men. He wondered how many other people had died on what appeared to have been a long and difficult journey.

Soon the guards yelled at the men and women. All stood instinctively and immediately. Atu stood and scanned the jungle for some sign of Kisi. She was obviously nowhere close.

Each of the men around Atu grabbed the wooden branch of another man and stood in a line. Atu grabbed the hanging yoke of the last man and they began walking south.

Atu looked around and saw many groups of five, six or seven men and women making their way through the jungle. No one was yelling or crying. He wondered how they'd been trained to be so quiet, then he remembered the bloody back of the dead man.

As they marched south, Atu knew they were heading to the coast. Within minutes the jungle rains began. The guards continued pushing the group in spite of the heavy rain and slippery conditions. It was then Atu knew how difficult it'd be for anyone to find their tracks. No one in the village was expecting them until dark and by morning most traces would be washed away.

It was hard to believe only hours earlier he'd told Kisi he was satisfied to remain in the jungle forever.

Chapter 10

April 15, 1777 – South Guinea – Fante Village

ATU'S father Ekow sat in the Fante village clearing with his wife Ejo. The afternoon sun had diminished and sunset was nearly upon them.

Ejo said, "It'll be a good thing to have Kisi for our son's wife. You've chosen well for him and I think she'll be a great mother to our grandchildren."

Ekow responded, "You seem to be in a hurry. They aren't even married and you're speaking of grandchildren. It's still four more days until the wedding feast and you're already dreaming."

She smiled and said, "There's nothing wrong in looking toward the future. If we live in the past, nothing changes. Change only comes in the future."

Atu's father said, "I'm surprised they aren't back yet. They must be enjoying themselves. I hope they're not enjoying themselves too much."

"They're young, but they're wise. They'll be careful. They won't disappoint us or our village."

Ekow looked up at the sky and said, "The sun is almost down and they aren't here."

"What could happen? This is our peaceful world."

"I'd agree, but I'm still concerned."

Kisi's parents, Kwaku and Mawusi arrived at the clearing. "Have you seen our children?"

"No, we've been waiting but haven't seen or heard anything. I'm beginning to worry."

It was dark. Ekow grabbed a torch of wrapped cloth, twigs and dead ferns from his hut and touched it to a hot coal from the cook fire. It erupted into flames and became a bright torch. He and Kisi's father walked the entire perimeter of the village looking for any sign of them.

There were many trails coming into the village and sadly they had no idea which direction their children had gone that morning.

Slowly walking back to their wives, they both felt a heavy weight.

Ejo asked, "Did you see anything?"

"No, nothing."

Ejo gasped. "What could have happened?"

Ekow responded, "There's nothing to do tonight. We have to believe our hunter son knows how to care for Kisi and himself. I think we'll have answers in the morning."

~

At first light, the village began another day. It wasn't long until the entire village heard that Atu and Kisi hadn't returned the night before. Ekow asked the large group which had gathered in the village clearing if anyone had seen the couple leave the morning before. No one had. Their hopes were crushed.

Ekow said, "We need to begin a search. Let's divide up into groups, move into the jungle and return at dusk. We know it rained yesterday and last night, so tracking will be nearly impossible. We should look for other signs."

The groups were selected and moved into the jungle in all directions. Ejo could hear the different groups calling the names of Atu and Kisi. As she sat with Kisi's mother in the clearing, they could hear the voices growing fainter and fainter. They waited quietly and hoped to hear an exuberant shouting from one of the groups indicating success. It didn't come, but dusk did, along with the disappointed and unsuccessful groups. Nothing. Nothing!

Ekow and Kisi's father returned. Ekow told Ejo, "It was very difficult. The rain wiped out the tracks. We didn't see anything that would give us a hint as to which direction they went. There's nothing to do now other than wait and see if they return or if someone learns something new. We have no idea what's happened."

Chapter 11

April 19, 1777 – *L'ange D'or* off the coast of Morocco

PIERRE had been five days at sea on his first ocean voyage. Overall it'd been going well. His routine and duties were set and he was getting his sea-legs. The first three days had been horrible as he'd lost his breakfast and dinner regularly over the side of the *L'ange D'or* gunwale. The crewmen had cheered every time it happened. They seemed to enjoy the cabin boy entertaining them. Gradually it got better, but the constant rolling and tossing of the ship in the waves and currents caused him to respect, as well as hate, the Atlantic.

The captain was kind to Pierre and the crew seemed to respect Captain Jean as a fair man. He was serious and uncompromising and Pierre knew that was needed for this motley crew of rabble.

The captain always had something to teach Pierre when they were together. Whether in the captain's quarters, in the galley or on deck, there was much to learn. The captain seemed to live up to the promises given to Pierre's mother, as he was keeping Pierre safe and at the same time educating him.

"Pierre my boy, come here."

Pierre joined the captain at the steering helm. "Put your hands on the wheel, lad."

Pierre grabbed the four foot mahogany wheel by two of its eight spokes. The captain opened the bittacle and showed the brass compass to Pierre. "See where the needle is pointing? The needle will always point to the north. Do you see how it's pointing directly behind us? That's because we're heading due south and true north is behind us. Now, I want you to hold the wheel steady and maintain a course due south. I'll be back soon."

Pierre stared at the captain who disappeared into the doorway of the stern leading to his quarters. The ocean was calm and the breeze steady, so it took little effort to maintain the course. A glance at the compass assured Pierre that all was good. He wondered how a captain could maintain a heading in the dark, or in the middle of a blinding torrent of rain, with thirty foot waves. His admiration for the captain grew.

Pierre looked down from the helm deck to the main deck to see Renard working with a coil of rope.

Renard smiled and winked, "Ahoy captain. Don't run us aground!"

Pierre looked away into the distance just as the captain arrived. The captain asked him, "Is everything good?"

He answered, "Yes, it's all good."

"Did you see any other ships, sand bars, whales or land while I was gone?"

Again it occurred to Pierre there was much more to captaining a ship than maintaining a proper course in good weather. He happily gave the wheel back to the captain.

Captain Jean said, "Look off to the port side of the ship."

Pierre turned to the open ocean on the right.

"No. You've just looked over the starboard side. Remember as you're facing the front of the ship, or the bow, forecastle and bowsprit, starboard will always be on your right and on the left will be port. Look out the port side."

Pierre looked left to see nothing but ocean. "Just beyond the horizon is Morocco. We've just passed the Gibraltar Straits separating Spain from Morocco. If we'd sailed through those straits, we could have visited Marseilles, France. It's a much larger port than Bordeaux."

The captain continued, "In twenty days, we'll arrive at Cape Coast port in Guinea, Africa. We'll be there eleven days unloading our cargo, bringing on more provisions, and loading the African cargo we'll take to Hispaniola in the Caribbean. Your education is only beginning!"

Pierre left the helm to continue his chores in the crew's forecastle galley at the bow.

The tables still held the dirty plates and utensils from the crew's morning breakfast. Rarely was food left on any of the plates as the crew was always ready to eat anything set in front of them. He began gathering the plates, mugs and utensils. He knew he needed to check the mugs for any leftover valuable water as it needed to be saved. It was a different thing after the evening meal, because there was never any liquid left in the mugs. That was when the crew received their daily ration of whiskey and brandy.

He was absorbed in gathering the items and failed to see a crewman entering the galley. Suddenly there was a large, heavy hand on his shoulder. Pierre recoiled and turned to see Renard.

"Oh. Did I startle you, captain's pet?"

"Yes. I thought I was alone."

"Yeah, you're alone. You're certainly correct about that!"

With that, Renard clamped a dirty, calloused hand over Pierre's mouth and wrapped his other arm around him. He picked Pierre up as if he weighed nothing, carried him to the side of the galley and threw him on the floor. Pierre struck his head on a post supporting the gunwale. Immediately blood appeared on his forehead. Groggily, he tried to fight against the weight of Renard. The hand over his mouth was smothering him. The blood from the cut was running into his eyes.

The blood shook Renard and he abruptly stood up. "Boy, you had better not tell anyone of this. I'll be watching. I'll see you again and there'd better be no fight left in you next time."

He left as quickly as he'd come.

Trembling and dazed, Pierre stood. He wiped the blood from his eyes and stumbled to a pail of water in the galley. Washing his face, he grabbed a towel and held it to his head. Sitting down on a bench, he waited. The bleeding didn't stop and seemed to be getting worse. He knew what he had to do.

He found the surgeon in his quarters in the forecastle. Looking at the injury, the surgeon said, "Son, I'll need to stitch this. That's a deep cut. What happened?"

Pierre paused, "I was working in the galley and slipped on the wet floor. I hit my head on a table."

The surgeon replied, "I'll need to tell the captain. You're his boy, you know. You wait here and I'll be back soon. He'll help with the sutures."

Pierre's fear came back. Renard was no one to cross. Soon the surgeon returned with the captain.

"The doctor told me what happened. That looks like a deep cut. I think you'll be taking a nice scar home to your mother. The surgeon said you bumped your head on a bucket hanging in the galley?"

Pierre was flustered and wasn't sure what to say. "Yeah, that's what happened."

"Okay, let's get this sewn up. The doctor will do a good job, but it'll hurt. These are the kinds of things that'll make you a man. Do you want a few sips of whiskey or brandy to take the edge off the pain?"

Pierre thought long and hard, "No, my mother wouldn't like that."

The surgeon retrieved the tools of his trade and said, "Laddie, your mother isn't here right now. I'd advise the whiskey, but it's your decision."

Pouring alcohol on a clean cloth, he cleaned the wound. The captain held Pierre's arms while the doctor sutured the cut.

"Pierre, you did very well. Not a whimper, scream or tears. I'm impressed."

Pierre frowned, "I think next time I'll take the whiskey."

~

Pierre walked into the morning sunshine and onto the main deck with the captain. Many of the men were working but stopped long enough to see the captain's cabin boy with a white bandage around his head.

Pierre made eye contact with Renard and quickly looked away. The captain followed Pierre's gaze and stared into the dark eyes of Renard.

Pierre went back to his duties. He couldn't help but worry about Renard and what might be his next plan. He was feeling a lot like a caged animal. There was simply no place to run or hide on board the ship. The only protection Pierre had was the captain. Since he'd just lied to him, the captain wasn't aware of the threats of Renard. Pierre knew Renard was likely wondering what he'd told the surgeon and captain. Well, there wasn't anything to do but tend to his duties and keep a watchful eye on Renard.

At high noon, the first mate asked Pierre to come to the captain's quarters. As he entered, he was surprised to see Renard sitting in a chair. The captain and second mate were standing nearby. Renard glared at Pierre.

The captain said, "I'd like to tell you all a story. When I was a small boy living in Paris, I had two older brothers. Our father brought home a puppy he'd found in an alley. He thought every boy should have a dog. The dog was small and full of life. Our family enjoyed him. However, one night the puppy wasn't in our yard where we kept him. My mother went outside and called for him. She found him under our steps. He was whimpering and cold and there was blood on his fur.

"My father took the shivering puppy, washed him and wrapped him in a warm blanket. He told us there were no holes in the fence for the dog to come or go. Nothing could come in and nothing could go out. Someone or something had hurt the puppy. Then he looked at each of his three boys. He told me to come and pet the dog. I did and the puppy licked my fingers. He asked my next older brother to do the same. Again, the same reaction. When my oldest brother reached out his hand, the puppy cowered in my father's arms.

"My dad asked us to leave him alone with my oldest brother. We did. My brother learned a hard lesson that day. One lesson was to treat animals and people with respect. The other lesson was that evil is nearly always found and dealt with.

"I tell you that story for a reason. Pierre, when you came on board the ship, I noticed Renard smiling at you and giving you a wink. This is not my first voyage and I know seafaring men better than I know my wife in Paris. I knew what that smile and wink meant. Earlier today, when we had to stitch your cut, you told the surgeon you had fallen and hit your head on a galley table. I decided to bait you. I told you the surgeon had said you bumped your head on a bucket hanging in the galley. You said that was correct. Those are two different stories. Pierre, if you're going to be a professional liar, you'll need more practice.

"Then, an hour ago when the surgeon was done, we came to the main deck. When you saw Renard, you quickly looked away. I saw the same look in you as I saw in our puppy when my older brother reached out to touch him. Then I looked to see who you had seen and I saw a look in Renard's eyes that told me the rest of the story."

The captain looked at Renard and asked him to stand. "Renard, did you hurt the boy?"

"No sir, I'd never do that. I'd never do anything like that!" Renard answered emphatically.

Captain Jean responded, "One thing I've learned over many voyages with many men is how to spot a liar.

"First Mate, take him to the main mast on deck."

The first mate grabbed Renard's arm and took him up the steps.

Grabbing a rope, he tied him face-first to the pole and stripped off his shirt. Then the captain called the crew.

The captain boomed, "We've a problem to deal with. I want to make seven things very clear. First, I'll tolerate no evil actions among the crew. Second, I know what goes on aboard my ship. Thirdly, this man devised evil toward my cabin boy Pierre and hurt him. Fourth, Pierre lied to protect Renard and himself. Fifth, I found out the truth by myself. Sixth, when I find evil doings, they are punished. Seventh, if the ten lashings today do not solve this problem, the next punishment for Renard is over the gunwale into the deep, dark, cold Atlantic."

The captain removed his own jacket and shirt. Pierre was amazed at the muscular build of the middle-aged man but was more amazed at the number of scars decorating the torso of Jean Moise. This was no man to take lightly. Pierre knew the captain wanted his men to see his torso, scars and willingness to discipline.

The captain was handed a whip by the first mate. The first lash brought blood, as did the remaining nine. To Renard's credit, there was no whimper or scream, though when released, he collapsed to the deck. As he lay on the deck, blood oozed out from under him. The message had been delivered. Pierre looked at Renard. There was no smile or wink.

The captain put on his shirt and jacket. Wiping his hands on Renard's discarded shirt, he walked to Pierre and said, "Let this be a lesson to you as well. Sometimes, evil needs to be brought into the light so it can be dealt with. You're fortunate to have someone as an advocate. I think your education this day has grown."

Chapter 12

April 20, 1777 – South Guinea

ATU had counted the days since he and Kisi had been captured. Five days had seemed like fifty. He had only one fleeting glimpse of her during those long day marches and was fairly certain she'd not seen him.

Aside from not having enough to eat or drink, Atu was doing well. Though the yoke around his neck was chafing and hurting he was surviving. As he watched the men in front of him, he realized they'd been on this journey for many weeks before he'd joined them, so he didn't have much to complain about.

The march had been uneventful, except for the deaths of two men who had been discarded as if they were monkey carcasses. Atu wondered how many bodies of men, women and children had littered the path on this jungle march.

The guards, though African, had no compassion or attachment to the 205 people they were responsible for herding south. Atu was careful about looking directly at the guards, but a discreet look saw complete indifference in their eyes. Likely, these men had been doing this for a long, long time.

He frantically wondered how Kisi was doing. Though he had no idea how much further they were going to travel, at least the two of them were still stronger than everyone else. That had to be a good thing.

Atu heard the splashing of water. As his small group of men moved forward, a large stream and pond opened to his view in a clearing. His group was prodded by the guards into the water. One of the guards used his hands to indicate this was their time to wash and get clean.

The men stumbled down the bank into the water. The water was fabulous. Atu couldn't help but smile as he scrubbed himself and soaked in the water. His mind wondered to five days earlier when he and Kisi had watched the elephants enjoying the same thing.

Quickly, the men were goaded out of the water and another group climbed in. It'd been refreshing and he felt clean and renewed.

The men were pushed into the jungle to rest until everyone had a chance to wash. Then it was back on their feet and the never-ending trek.

Something seemed to be changing. It'd been so subtle he'd been almost unaware. As he plodded through the jungle, he noticed a change in the air. Was it the breeze, or was it a smell, or both?

He'd been accustomed to the humidity of the rain forest and jungle, but it was now different. Though there was a breeze, the heat was increasing and the air had a peculiar smell to it. It was sultry, almost salty.

An hour later he heard a new noise. At first the sound was almost imperceptible but then it gradually increased. He was now able to hear a faint crashing that came and went.

The large group began emerging from the diminishing trees and stared at a scene unimaginable for someone who had always lived in a jungle.

Ahead to his left was a large village. There were huts as far as he could see. To the right were rocky ridges and a bare landscape. Beyond the rocks was a body of water that seemingly went on forever.

But, the most captivating thing was a white building that stretched out in front of him. There were windows from the top to the bottom. He saw large walls with arched walkways. It was huge!

He continued staring and taking in the view. The building was something he could never have imagined. Likewise, the African village seemed large enough to hold many more people than he imagined possible.

He looked behind him and saw his group. The weakest and most emaciated of the group were staring at the same scene. Everyone was captivated.

During the march, guards were only responsible for small groups finding their way through the dense forest and jungle. Now, everyone was together. Atu was amazed at the size of the group. He had no idea there were so many men and women as this was the first time they were grouped together.

He desperately searched for Kisi. He couldn't see her in the group. When he was about to give up, he saw her at the far end!

"Kisi," he yelled.

Immediately he was hit with the butt of a spear that knocked him to the ground.

He laid there with a heart full of thanksgiving knowing Kisi was safe. The guard kicked him and motioned for him to stand.

The guards began organizing the group. The children were first. It was the saddest thing Atu had ever seen. Several dozen children, from probably eight to twelve-years-old were all tied together with ropes around their necks. All of them were in single file. A few were crying. All looked fearful.

Atu watched as the children were herded and prodded toward the white building. Then the guards pushed the women into a single line following the children. Some of the women were the mothers of the children in front. He couldn't imagine what they were feeling as they watched their children heading into the unknown. He saw Kisi and his heart nearly skipped a beat wondering if he'd ever see her again. Surely this wouldn't be the last time he'd see his fiancé?

Then the men were maneuvered into single file, following the women. As the long line of Africans moved south toward the shoreline, they entered the large clearing between the huge white building and the village.

~

Kisi was terrified as the women walked slowly toward the shoreline. She and Atu had been talking about the ocean only five days ago. Her heart ached as she thought of her mother and father and the horrible tragedy that had been thrust upon her village. What were they thinking? What were they doing? She knew her father wouldn't simply accept the loss of his only daughter. She knew he'd do something. But, what could he do?

She'd been so happy to see Atu two different times in the last five days. He appeared to be doing well and that made her hopeful. Then, she remembered yesterday was to have been their wedding day and feast. That thought brought the silent tears flowing down her cheeks once again.

Kisi looked at the Guinea village off to her left. It started near the shoreline and stretched back to the forest. It seemed to go east until swallowed up by small hills. African people were everywhere.

She couldn't believe the villagers weren't even watching this group of Africans being brought to the white building. It was almost as if they didn't exist. She felt like an invisible ghost. Why weren't people doing something to help them? Life was going on as normal for these villagers. Maybe that was the problem. This was their norm. Was it possible they'd seen this before? Maybe, many, many times?

Kisi looked ahead as the children entered a narrow doorway of the white building. They disappeared into the darkness. As the single line continued funneling into the doorway, it was soon to be Kisi's turn.

She was twenty feet away, then ten, then five and then she entered the darkness. Holding the yoke shank of the woman ahead of her, she stumbled as her feet tried to navigate the rough stone floor. Kisi wondered how the children fared as they walked into this darkness. The smell was musty and wet. The sounds of shuffling feet filled the quietness of the walkway. She felt like she was entering a tomb and she shuddered involuntarily. Her shoulder brushed against the wet wall. They walked for thirty feet and turned right into another hallway with a light at the end.

Emerging through the end of the hallway, Kisi entered a courtyard. The children were nowhere to be seen. She could hear the children screaming and crying somewhere. The sounds were muffled and terrifying. The mothers became frantic so the guards whipped some of the women. The screaming and crying continued from deep inside the building.

Then, Kisi saw something she'd never seen before. Her mouth literally dropped open and an involuntary gasp escaped. She saw men who were white! She had no idea anyone could look like that. Sometimes Fante villagers covered themselves in ashes for their dancing, but this was different. The skin on these men was white. It was the most bizarre thing she'd ever seen.

Now the captured African men arrived through the door and entered the courtyard. Kisi saw Atu. She watched the reactions of the African men as they viewed the white men. It was no different than her own.

Who were these strange men and more importantly what did they want from the African men, women and children?

A fire was burning in the center of the courtyard. Three white men were tending it. Steel rods were sticking out of the fire. Two guards began removing the wooden shackle yokes from the first women.

Two white men stood in front of the first woman and were making marks in a book. Then they moved to the second woman. Were all the people inside the white building white men?

Another guard took the first woman to the fire. Two held her tightly by her arms while a third pulled a red-hot iron rod from the fire. He pushed it against the woman's shoulder on her back. She screamed.

A guard took her to another part of the courtyard where a pile of iron chains were laying. A man locked an iron clasp around her ankle which had a four foot iron chain and hook attached. They forced her to grasp the chain in her hand and she was led to another area of the yard.

After sixty or so women had been processed, it was time for Kisi to walk to the fire. She was desperate, but she was Fante and her fiancé was watching. Bravely she walked to the fire with her head held high. Gritting her teeth, she watched as the man pulled the iron from the fire. It was red hot. Kisi could see there was a design on the bottom which would be branded onto her back. The man raised the iron and pushed it against her skin. She heard the sizzle, almost like the sound she'd heard when dropping greasy bongo meat into the boiling water of her village stew. The pain was intense. She wanted to scream but Fante pride gripped her tongue and lips. She knew Atu was watching and she knew he was proud.

The cycle of women from the line continued until the last woman had been unshackled, counted, documented, branded and re-shackled.

The women were then pushed toward another dark doorway. Entering, they shuffled through the darkness. Kisi could tell the hallway was curving to the right and was gradually going lower and lower. They entered a large semi-dark room. The walls were mortared with stones and bricks. The ceiling of the room was arched and very high. The boys and girls were in this room. The guards removed the ropes from their necks and permitted them to reunite with their mothers.

Kisi wept as she watched the reunion. Some of the children hadn't been with their mothers for the entire trip through the jungles, forests and plains.

The guards pushed the mothers and children to one side of the large dungeon.

~

Atu nearly screamed out as he watched Kisi getting branded. But, he swelled with pride as he watched his fiancé bravely accept the inevitable. She was the woman the ancestors had brought to his side. Or was she? What was their destiny? Would they ever be together?

The women had disappeared into the dark mouth of the building once again. The process of unshackling, documenting, counting, branding and re-shackling the men continued. He received his brand like a man. The iron shackle was secured around his neck and the four foot chain and hook dangled in front of him.

After all the men had been processed, the guards moved the men through the same dark doorway into which the women had disappeared.

Slowly shuffling downward and forward, they came to a large room filled with women and children. Atu recognized them as his traveling companions but he couldn't see Kisi. The group was packed tightly. They were quiet as they watched the men lumbering past with clanking chains. No one dared utter a word.

They continued downward. The smell of the dark, dank and wet dungeons was horrible. He gagged as did many others.

They passed another room filled with more women and children. Finally, there were a few chambers filled with men. It became darker and darker. Finally at the bottom, they stopped.

There were two small openings twelve to fifteen feet from the floor that let in slivers of light. The light permitted him to see a hundred or so men in this lower level.

Shuffling into the chamber, his feet became wet. As he went further into the room, his ankles were submerged. The stench was horrible. A man gagged and vomited and then Atu knew what some of the liquid on the floor was.

The guards left. Atu tried to move toward a wall. He knew soon he'd be tired and he desperately didn't want to sit in whatever was on the floor. As he elbowed his way forward, he was amazed at how weakly these men resisted him. How long had they been here?

Soon, he reached a wet, slimy and cool wall. He kept moving along it until his ankles were no longer submerged. He leaned against the wall and waited. He had no idea what he was waiting for.

Finally, there was some murmuring and whispering among the large group. The guards had left, so the captives were able to communicate. It was then he heard a Fante word, and then a phrase. He listened and tried to pinpoint where it'd come from. As anxious as he was to find another Fante in this group, he knew this cool and stable wall was more precious than talking to another man. He waited.

Chapter 13

April 21, 1777 – Cape Coast Castle – The Gold Coast of Guinea

THE night had been long and difficult. Several times Atu had gagged and vomited from the stench. The retching was an ongoing sound throughout the night.

Atu finally gave in to his bodily functions and defecated and urinated into the liquid cesspool that had now become part of his life.

The stench was more than feces, urine and vomit. Atu smelled rotting flesh. He knew somewhere within this group of weak and sick men, some must have died. Somewhere in this hell were dead and decaying men. Atu involuntarily pulled his feet back from the slime beneath him in a futile effort to escape it. He'd seen rotting flesh in the jungle and knew it quickly became alive with maggots and larvae lodging in the dead flesh.

Being in the bottom chamber of the dungeon made it the recipient for whatever liquids wanted to find their way downward. Atu wondered how deep this cesspool would get before he was removed. Would he be removed? When? What would be next? It couldn't get any worse than this. Could it?

Then, there it was. The Fante language again. Closer this time. In Fante, Atu said, "I am Fante."

Then, several voices answered.

Soon, someone found their way to his voice. The man said, "I am Fante." They touched hands and embraced.

As there were many Fante throughout southern Guinea, there had been little chance of them knowing one another or even knowing of one another's villages. But they felt like brothers with their common language and customs.

Atu asked, "What's your name?"

"Kwessi."

"My name is Atu. How long have you been here?"

"It's nearly impossible to know. The little light coming in at the top can give us an idea so I'd guess it's been thirty or forty days. Others have been here longer. Some for three months."

Atu was shocked at what he was hearing. How could he survive this hell for that long?

He asked Kwessi, "Why are we here?"

Kwessi paused a moment and began, "We've been kidnapped to become slaves. Most of us don't know anything other than what we've heard from others.

"Some of it is rumor and some of it's probably fact. It's difficult to tell the difference. Some believe we've been kidnapped to be eaten by the white men. I doubt that's true. Another man said he saw African people in small wooden boats being taken out to a large ship on the ocean. I think that's true."

He continued, "All of us are waiting for something to happen. The longer I'm waiting, the more I realize the thing that'd bring me the most pleasure is death."

They continued talking about their life in the villages where they'd been raised. For both, it seemed a lifetime ago.

~

Kisi sat on the floor of the dungeon chamber. It was dark. The two small holes at the ceiling left in a little light. She'd watched the light diminish last evening. Gradually this morning, it pushed its way slowly into their midst. There were no toilets provided so they tried to keep an area separated for that purpose though Kisi watched the urine flow downward to somewhere lower in this series of dungeons.

She'd found a thirty-year-old Fante woman in the group and learned her name was Adzo. They spent time talking together and it was very comforting to have someone to communicate with. They held hands the entire time they talked.

While Kisi and Adzo were talking earlier that morning, a white man had appeared in the hallway. Adzo immediately cringed and tried to hide behind another woman. The man had a torch burning and walked carefully among the women. He grabbed the wrist of a woman about twenty-years-old and pulled her toward the hall. She disappeared around the corner with him.

Adzo was trembling and Kisi asked, "What's wrong? What just happened?"

With a quivering voice, Adzo said, "This happens every day. A woman or two from our group are selected by a white guard. They're taken up to the courtyard, washed and taken into the upper part of the big building to white men. She's forced to spend time with them and then they're returned."

Kisi waited and then asked, "Adzo, how do you know what happens to them? Has this happened to you?"

"Yes, four times. We're just one group of women in these many dungeons. Others are in another area. I've passed by them on my way to the upper parts. I think this is happening to many women and girls."

"How long have you been here?"

"I'm not sure, but maybe eighty days." Then she stopped talking and began crying.

Kisi asked, "What's wrong? Why are you crying?"

Through her tears, she mumbled, "I think I'm pregnant from the white men in the building."

She continued, "The first time I was selected by a guard was terrifying. I'd heard the white men ate Africans and that was why we were here. So, I thought the white men's appetites would take me to their cooking fires. It's true they have appetites for African flesh but not in the cooking pots.

"When I was selected, I was washed and then taken up a stairway to an area close to the top of the building. A white man took me into his home. I walked past his beautiful furniture and trays of food. There were many windows facing the ocean and it was beautiful. The sunshine came in through the windows and the breeze was wonderful. The salty air smelled fresh and the sound of the crashing waves was peaceful. I saw white women in the courtyard and children playing. It's a very different world than the dungeons. Everyone was clean and well fed. I couldn't believe it.

"When the white man was finished with me, a guard took me to other rooms and other men. Then he brought me back to the dungeon and my horrible life kept getting worse.

"Kisi, I'll do all I can to keep you out of sight when the man comes back. Stay behind me and low to the ground. You don't want to make that trip to the white men's Castle."

Adzo continued to share things she'd heard about why they were here and what their future might be. But, the worst part was not knowing the truth. The rumors created a lot of fear.

Chapter 14

May 2, 1777 – *L'ange D'or* off the coast of Sierra Leone, Africa

EIGHTEEN days aboard the *L'ange D'or* had changed Pierre. He was bronzed from the ceaseless sun and he was certainly getting an education, just as the captain had predicted. He laid in his bunk, letting his mind wander while waiting for sleep.

Renard had left him alone. The men aboard ship had actually shown Pierre respect and contempt for Renard. Whatever Renard had within his soul, the other men didn't want it for themselves.

Renard had replaced his wink and smile with a glare. That made Pierre equally uncomfortable, but he knew the captain and crew had his back. Pierre continued to be wary. That in itself likely wasn't a bad thing. Not naively trusting everyone he came in contact with was probably a good life lesson.

Pierre wondered how his mother was getting along. The two of them had drawn close in the absence of his father. He'd almost forgotten this was the ship his father had been on when the accident had occurred. He was glad the captain had shown him his father's watery grave.

A light flickered in the hallway and the captain appeared with a candle. He stopped at Pierre's bunk and asked, "Pierre, did you have a good day?"

"Yes sir, I did."

"Good. You've been doing a fine job. We've been at sea for eighteen days and only have seven or so to go. Unless we have bad weather, we'll likely arrive in Africa on May 9th."

Pierre thought a moment and asked, "Captain, I was wondering if you'd ever sailed with my father before?"

"Did you mean any other trips before the one where he lost his life? Yes, I did. I think he was with me three times."

"What was he like? I knew him as a father, but now that I'm aboard your ship I've wondered what he was like as a sailor... and as a man?"

With a wink, the captain said, "Ah, that's a great question to ask. I'm surprised to hear it from such a young man. Tell you what, come into my quarters so I can sit down. I'm getting older and I like to sit when I can."

Then the captain said, "Sorry about the wink, my boy, I trust you know, a wink coming from me means something entirely different than from Renard."

Pierre smiled.

In the captain's quarters, Pierre sat on one of the chairs. The captain went to a small box on a shelf and retrieved something wrapped in paper.

Handing it to Pierre, he said, "See what you think of this candy."

Pierre unwrapped it and looked at the amber colored sweet. The captain said, "Soon we'll be in Hispaniola and you'll be able to see the sugarcane plantations. When sugarcane is pressed and boiled it creates crystals of sugar. The candy you're holding are those crystals, along with honey and nuts. Try it."

Pierre put it in his mouth and relished the sweetness of something new to him.

"Now, back to your question regarding your father. As I mentioned, I think he sailed with me three times. The last time you know about. There are men who sail because they like the adventure on the high seas. There are others who enjoy the foreign ports. Many stay in those ports and never return. There are those who do it for the money, the liquor and the life it brings. Your father did it for the money and not for the liquor and what that brought. He did it for your mother and you. He was very unique in that sense. Because of his principles and values, he was not always treated well by the crew. They tended to laugh at him because of him being honorable and how he valued his family. Most men aboard my ship lost their families years ago. Or more accurately, they were disowned. I think some of the crew were jealous of your father."

Pierre smiled as he thought of this side of his father. He was looking forward to telling his mother what he was learning.

Captain Jean continued. "I think he'd be very displeased to know you were on this ship. But, if he knew how well you were doing, I think he'd be very proud of you.

"Well, it's getting late and this old man needs to get some sleep."

"Thanks sir for sharing. I'm learning more about who my father was now that he's gone, than while he was alive."

~

The next morning, Pierre hurried through his work and headed to the helm. The captain was taking his turn at the wheel. It seemed to Pierre he was always willing to talk.

Pierre looked at the compass and noticed they were gradually moving into the southeast. "Captain, I see we're beginning to change course?"

"Yes, the coast of Africa is off the port side about thirty miles. If we put ashore here we'd land in Sierra Leone, Africa. We'd enter a harbor in a large bay. You'd be surprised to see how many ships would be there as it's a very large port for trade. Other ships will go there to unload their cargo and then carry men and women to the America's and Caribbean for work. But our African port is further south and then east."

Pierre said, "So, the people who are carried to the America's and Caribbean for work come from this part of Africa?"

"Yes. The New World is ripe for development. The America's, both north and south have a great need for workers. The Portuguese, Spanish, French, English and Dutch all need workers for the Caribbean. When the islands were founded, they were inhabited by native Indians who were quickly enslaved as workers. Unfortunately it didn't take long for the European diseases to kill the Indians. When the European workers tried to take the Indian's place and work in the hot climates, they soon died from malaria and other diseases. So, African workers are being used to replace the Indians. They'd lived in hot equatorial climates and were able to withstand the harsh environments of the Caribbean. It was a perfect fit. Since the 1500's, hundreds of thousands of African men and women have been transported to those countries for work."

Pierre said, "It must cost a huge amount of money to transport so many people so far? Who pays for that?"

"Ah, another great question. The answer is what we call the Atlantic Trade Triangle. You know that a triangle has three legs. In the Atlantic Trade Triangle, the first leg on the map would run south from Europe to the Gold Coast where we'll be in five days. The second leg goes northwesterly from the Gold Coast to the Caribbean and the America's. The last leg is from the Caribbean and the America's and runs a northeasterly course back to Europe.

"On the first leg, ship loads of trinkets, guns, knives, rum, brandy, whiskey, cloth and countless other items are carried from the factories of Europe and England to the African coastal colonies and forts on the Gold and Ivory coasts.

"There they'll be sold or traded for the African workers who will be going to the Caribbean and America's. That's the beginning of the second leg of the triangle. When the ships arrive in the Caribbean or America's, the workers are unloaded. The money received from their sale then purchases items to take back to Europe where the cycle starts all over again. Products like tobacco, refined sugar, rum, indigo ink and many other things are transported back. At each stop, the owners of the ships make a profit. This business is extremely profitable for the shipping company owners, plantation owners and all the others who profit from the products that are made and sold. This triangle provides jobs for sailors and many other people, including Africans."

With a puzzled look, Pierre said, "You mentioned that the workers are unloaded in the Caribbean or America's and money is received from their sale. What are you saying?"

"The Africans are slave laborers. They're poor and simple people. In addition, they're uncivilized in the jungles. They don't have factories or industry like those of us from Europe and England. When we take them to the Caribbean, they see what we've been able to accomplish. They've never seen anything like it. Fortunately for them, they're brought into a Christian environment in the Caribbean and America's. It's a blessing for them to be removed from their pagan gods. Our churches are supportive of this charitable outreach to them, but not always pleased with how it's carried out. Some people may call it slavery, but we as Christians bring them to Christianity and civilization."

The captain continued, "God's created everything. One of the things He's created are the trade winds. Some say the easterly trade winds blowing from Africa to the America's are a blessing and affirmation from God to us. The success of the Atlantic Trade Triangle happens because of the winds. He's made it easy for us to make the trip with full sails. Literally He's behind us."

Pierre didn't know what to say, so he responded, "I'm looking forward to seeing Africa and meeting the people. I suppose it'll be another part of my education."

Chapter 15

DARIFA was getting weaker. It had been thirty-five days on the horrible march through the jungles. She'd thought it couldn't get any worse. Now it was already another fifteen days of captivity at the white men's Castle. Then, things got worse.

An African guard entered her dungeon chamber with his blazing torch. The women and girls cowered, trying to become invisible in the crowd as he drew closer. He walked past Darifa, reached the end of the dismal chamber and then slowly walked back toward her. He stopped in front of her and grabbed her wrist. Yanking her to her feet he pulled her up the ramp.

In the courtyard she was given soap and a bucket of water to bathe. Though it had been refreshing to be clean again and invigorating to be in the fresh, warm coastal air, she knew from the experiences of others what was yet to come. The bath and fresh air weren't a gift. There was a price to pay and nothing good was to come of this. The guard gave her a dress to wear.

Following behind the African guard, she climbed a set of stairs to the next floor above the courtyard. She heard strange singing as they walked past a large room. A glimpse revealed a room full of white men and women dressed formally. They were singing slow songs which had no resemblance to her own native music.

At the end of the balcony hallway they took another set of stairs upward. There, the guard unlocked a door and pushed Darifa into a small room. He shut the door and she heard a heavy steel rod slam into place. She sat on the only chair in the room and looked around.

There was nothing else in the room. Her anxiety grew as she waited and waited. She listened to the faint singing. It seemed to go on forever. Then it stopped.

After ten minutes, she heard someone shuffling past. Another ten minutes passed until the steel rod was removed and a man stood in the doorway. He was as white as the shirt he wore and was wearing an open black coat that reached his knees. He wore pants that stopped also at his knees and his bottom legs were covered in white material. His hair was white.

He said something to Darifa and motioned her to follow him. She followed him down the balcony hallway to a door. Outside the door was another white man who was obviously a guard. The white haired man opened the door and went in. She followed.

She raised her head enough to look around. Furniture and food were abundant. She looked to the right and was startled to see the face of a black woman. Hanging on the wall was a flat piece of shiny material that reflected anything in front of it. She stared. What stared back wasn't the young woman she'd seen in the still water of her village stream. This woman was older, sad and haggard.

On the wall beside the reflected image was a different kind of image. It was a painted scene of the white-haired white man, a woman and three children. Darifa knew this was a man of importance.

He led Darifa into the next room.

Emerging thirty minutes later the guard led her down the stairs, past the now empty room where the singing had been and down another stairs. He led her across the courtyard through the dark doorway and hallway where he took her dress.

Then the guard reached for her...

Ten minutes later, the smell of the dungeons caught her breath as they descended lower into the earth. Reaching her group, she sat on the floor and wept.

Kisi sat amidst the mass of women and girls in the dungeon. Earlier, she'd watched the guard with the torch trying to select a woman for the man upstairs. Kisi had cowered with the rest of the girls and women and was thankful she wasn't selected. When she saw the man select and take Darifa, she felt guilty for the relief she'd just felt.

Now she heard the sobs of Darifa and knew she needed to seek her out.

She began moving through the hundred or so women in her group. It was difficult to see anyone in the dark. Periodically, the small light from the ceiling created a flicker in terrified eyes and Kisi got a glimpse of her companions. She couldn't find Darifa.

Finally, exasperated, she took a chance and said, "Darifa." Everyone grew quiet. Then she heard a voice at the far end respond, "Kisi."

Kisi moved in the direction of the voice. Again, "Darifa." She was startled to have someone grab her arm in the dark.

Kisi and Darifa embraced. For fear of a beating or lashing, they could only whisper. They both wept.

Chapter 16

May 8, 1777 – South Guinea – Fante Tribe

EKOW and Ejo, Atu's parents, were desperate and devastated, as were Kisi's parents Kwaku and Mawusi in the disappearance of their son and daughter. The twenty-three days since Atu and Kisi had disappeared were a time of mourning for the entire village. For over a week, a few villagers had entered the jungle seeking clues as to what had happened to them. Each day they returned with no clues and less hope.

All the villagers were losing hope. Ekow and Kwaku had gone out together this morning and were searching west of their village. They came upon two men moving south through the jungle.

Though from another part of central Guinea, they all understood Fante.

One of the strangers greeted the two fathers and said, "I seek forgiveness for walking on your tribal land."

Kwaku said, "No, this is not our land. We're strangers here as well. Our village lies much further to the east."

The man asked, "Why are you here in this place? Are you hunting?"

"Hunting, yes. But not for bongo or warthog. We're searching for our son and daughter. They disappeared twenty-three days ago. They were to be married and had taken a walk together. They never returned."

The strangers were surprised. "We're searching for four men from our tribe as well. They've been gone for twenty-seven days. We searched and searched but haven't found any sign of them. Then three days ago, African traders from the north told us of a large group of people who had been captured many weeks ago north of us. They were being taken to the south coast. There's a place there where men and women are taken across the ocean as slaves. They told us this was the path. We've seen signs along the way of trees cut down and foliage destroyed so we're continuing to the coast."

The stranger continued, "Come with us. We'll show you something."

Ekow and Kwaku followed the men north for ten minutes to a clearing. There they saw small trees which had been cut and the brush and ferns had been damaged in several large areas. The man continued, "We think this was an area where a large group rested.

"Come with us, we'll show you more."

Twenty paces further they stopped. They pulled back the grass to expose the decomposing remains of a person. It was obvious the body had been eaten by animals and birds.

Kwaku said, "What's that wooden piece around his neck? It looks like a wooden tool."

Ekow lifted the wooden apparatus until they saw it'd been a shackle of some sort.

Ekow asked the two men, "Can you tell us more about where you think the group is going?"

"We believe it's south from here."

Memorizing the location, Ekow looked up at the sky and around the surrounding area. He looked at Kwaku. "We need to go back to our village and gather supplies for the journey."

Looking at the two strangers, he said, "Thanks for giving us this information. We've been without hope. We might see you soon at the coast. Safe journey."

The two strangers continued south while Kwaku and Ekow moved quickly toward their village in the eastern jungle.

After thirty minutes, they entered their village. Sharing the new information with their wives, they each gathered a small bag filled with dried meat. Whatever else they needed, they'd find on the way.

Immediately, the two fathers, headed back west toward the path which would take them south and hopefully to the location of Atu and Kisi.

The Fante villagers had new hope.

Chapter 17

May 10, 1777 – *L'ange D'or* at Cape Coast Port, Guinea, Africa

SUNRISE on board the three masted cargo ship *L'ange D'or* was always a busy time. This was the day they were to arrive at Cape Coast port, Guinea, Africa, so there was much to do.

The captain was at the helm at noon, so Pierre joined him. "Captain, when will we arrive at Cape Coast port?"

"My boy, you're anxious to get your feet on dry land?"

"Yeah, that sounds great. Twenty-five days at sea has been a long time."

"There are times we're at sea much longer. Our trip to Hispaniola can sometimes take ninety days depending on the weather. A few ships have been known to make the crossing in under fifty days, but the fastest I've ever made it is eighty days. Some ships only carry a hundred people for the crossing, but we'll be carrying almost five hundred including the crew. That'll be a heavy ship considering all the provisions and cargo we're also carrying."

He continued, "Come back to the helm when your work's done at four this afternoon. I think we'll see land then. We'll stay on board the ship tonight and go to shore in the morning to make arrangements for unloading the ship."

Pierre was excited and quickly went about his chores. Four o'clock came quickly and he was at the helm at exactly four.

The captain laughed as he pulled out his pocket-watch and saw the time. "You're an anxious lad, aren't you?"

Pierre laughed. The captain gave him a small brass telescope which Pierre quickly adjusted and put to his eye. It wasn't the first time he'd used one. Several times on the voyage, the captain had let him observe whales and other passing ships.

Several days earlier when they'd passed Sierra Leone, they'd seen several ships coming and going toward the harbor and bay. Pierre had asked the captain what they were carrying. The captain looked at them through the telescope and said, "Those going into port are carrying cargo such as our own. The ones leaving are slavers."

"How do you know they're slave ships?"

The captain gave him the glass and said, "Do you see the white canvas alongside the ship? On the main deck, there are sails on the main, fore and mizzen masts, but look at the ones on the sides of the ship."

Pierre said, "Yeah, I see them."

"Those small sails aren't actually sails to move the ship. They're fastened alongside to catch the wind and divert it into the holds to cool the African cargo. That's one way to identify a slaver heading to the New World."

Pierre was appreciating this learning process, but there were questions he had which he chose not to ask. Just now the captain had said 'African cargo'. It seemed some men considered the Africans as something other than human. Pierre didn't understand how a good, educated and experienced man like the captain could talk about another human being as he did.

With his eye to the glass, Pierre hollered, "Land Ho!"

He'd just seen the rocky shore of Cape Coast. As they closed the distance, he saw the masts of many ships in the harbor. One was going to pass close by the *L'ange D'or* soon. As he continued looking at the shoreline, he saw a huge white building.

"Captain, what's that large building?"

"That's the Cape Coast Castle. Up and down this African Atlantic seaboard coast there are forty or so castles and forts in several countries. The Cape Coast Castle was first built by the Swedes in the 1650's. Over the next twenty or so years it was taken and re-taken by various countries until England took it over in the 1660's. It's still British today.

"This long coast line has various names depending on where you might be. We've already passed the Grain and Ivory Coasts. Guinea, which you see over the port side, is along the Gold Coast and what we call the Slave Coast further east. All the names indicate things of high value. Grain, ivory, gold and slaves are expensive products and produce a lot of revenue. Due to them, the forts and castles have been the trading places for many years. The grain, ivory and gold is actually of much less value now than the slaves. The white building which is called a castle, is the temporary home to over one thousand African men and women waiting for ships. That's where our cargo is stored."

"Captain, I was wondering about something you said. You said we'd be taking almost five hundred people to the Caribbean. I didn't think this ship could even hold one hundred. Where will they all go?"

"My, you certainly have a lot of questions. They'll be answered by your own eyes in the next few weeks. But, trust me. Ship captains know how to stow their cargo. You'll see."

The outbound ship with England's flag was starboard about two hundred yards. Pierre could clearly see men on board waving at them next to their deck cannons. But, he didn't see any Africans. He knew they were aboard as he saw the side canvas capturing the breeze for their benefit. He was thankful the British crew cared enough about their African cargo to keep them comfortable.

They were approaching the harbor and Pierre was astonished at what he saw. To the starboard side was a large village which he presumed was for Africans. He counted eight large ships in the harbor. There were a number of small wooden boats trekking back and forth between the large ships and the shore. Nearly capturing the entire landscape in front of the *L'ange D'or* was the huge white building. He saw countless black cannons on the bulwarks of the high white rock walls. The building had three or four levels. The entire place was a fortress and magnificent. It was a castle.

The captain startled him when he said with his booming voice, "Drop the starboard anchor!"

Pierre watched as the men scrambled to the starboard bow. One man removed a wooden plug from the gunwale. A group of crewmen brought a large coil of heavy rope from below-deck. They began uncoiling it by laying it down on the main deck almost from bow to stern. Then again and again they made the trip fore and aft to untwist it until soon the entire rope was loosened and ready to attach to the anchor through the gunwale.

Another crewman brought an empty wooden barrel from below and attached it loosely to the rope outside the bow of the ship. The rope was attached ship-side to strong beams. The other end was attached to the anchor which was lashed to the starboard side of the ship.

The rope was nearly three times longer than the depth of water they were in. With the command to drop the anchor, the ropes holding the anchor to the bow were loosened and the anchor dropped. As it sunk, the barrel buoy continued to slip up the anchor line. When the anchor grounded, the buoy marked its spot.

Pierre noticed the wind was pushing the ship backwards away from the buoy and anchor. Immediately the crew was commanded to ready the port bow anchor for dropping. The process happened again, only more quickly. The first anchors rope was now taut and holding the ship. The sails had been lowered to prevent undue pressure on the starboard side anchor.

The port anchor was dropped with another buoy. When grounded, the captain ordered the crew to man the capstan reel to bring in some of the bow anchor ropes. When the ship was midway between the two anchors, the job was completed.

Pierre had no idea the job was so complex or that the crew could accomplish so much in such a short period of time. His respect and admiration for the captain was growing on a daily basis.

"Captain. That was a lot of hard work. Why didn't you just use one anchor?"

"Sometimes a job is more difficult than what some think it should be. An inexperienced eye is usually looking for shortcuts. There are always reasons for what we do, when we do it and how it's done. In this case, if we only used one anchor, the winds and currents would push us around it in a circle. With two, we're secure in case of a storm or wild currents. Your questions tell me you have a sharp and inquisitive mind. I think Pierre, you'll be a success in life no matter what you choose to do."

Pierre liked the new knowledge, but he absolutely loved the affirmation and respect the captain threw his way.

Pierre focused his attention on the shore. He picked up the brass scope once again and viewed the shoreline.

Small wooden boats were being loaded with black men and women on the beach. He watched as one boat was pushed off shore into the surf. He thought they'd capsize when the bow of the boat raised skyward only to come crashing down behind the wave. Again and again it happened until they were twenty yards from shore. Then they set course on calm water for a ship in the bay.

The ship had a flag Pierre didn't recognize. He gave the scope to the captain and asked him who the ship belonged to. The captain said, "That's a Portuguese ship belonging to a textile merchant in Lisbon. Twenty-two years ago a horrible earthquake almost demolished the city. Merchants had to change their markets and products. The ship's owner decided to sell abroad rather than locally due to Lisbon's wealth being decimated by the quake. He's been moving his products to Africa and the Caribbean. The name of the ship is *Gloria de Deus*. It means *Glory of God.* The captain is a friend of mine. Captain Arsenio.

He's taking his cargo to the same Caribbean island to which we're sailing. The island of Hispaniola is French on the west side, where we'll go. It's Spanish to the east, where Captain Arsenio will sail."

Pierre continued watching through the scope as a series of ropes and ladders were lowered over the side of the *Gloria de Deus*. The Africans began climbing aboard. He could see crewmen using whips to direct the Africans. He couldn't hear the snap, but Pierre could almost feel the lash as he remembered what had happened to Renard.

He looked back to the shore and saw another small boat between shore and the Portuguese cargo ship. There was yet another being loaded on the beach. There were still many more black men and women sitting on the sand.

Pierre scanned the other seven ships in the harbor. It seemed they were all waiting for something. Money wasn't being made by keeping ships in a harbor. He knew the ships were here to unload freight and pick up cargo. He said, "Captain, how many of the eight ships in the bay are picking up African slaves?"

"All of them. Black gold is the product being moved from this port. This castle at Cape Coast is here for only one reason. To collect and process workers for the America's and the Caribbean. There are ports from the very north of North America at Boston, to the southern parts of Brazil in South America. There are countless other ports in those two continents as well as in the Caribbean."

Pierre looked puzzled. "Why are you calling the African slaves Black Gold?"

The captain said with a laugh, "I'm sorry. Yes, Black Gold. Guinea had a lot of yellow gold in the 1400's through the 1600's but most of it was mined and sold. The new gold coming from Cape Coast Castle are the African workers we're transporting. It's different than the gold of the 1500's. That gold ran out. This Black Gold is a never-ending supply, and it's much more valuable than the yellow."

The crew was working hard to ready the ship for unloading, so Pierre headed back to his work. The captain was keeping a skeleton crew on board tomorrow morning to secure the ship. Most of the men would have a day on shore and from observing how hard the crew was working, they were very anxious for the leave.

The business of readying the ship for unloading fell to the experienced crew. Pierre spent his time in the forecastle galley preparing food for the crew's supper.

The captain had told Pierre, "You'll leave the ship with me in the morning. I've told your mother I'd keep you safe. Though the Africans aren't civilized, here on the coast they're usually gentle people. You probably have more to worry about with a drunken crew than you do with wild animals or Africans."

When the crew began arriving below deck, the atmosphere in the galley was full of excitement. He listened to the men's conversation. His father had once told him, "Pierre, God gave you two ears and one mouth. You should listen twice as much as you talk."

As he moved from one table to another, he heard bits and pieces of conversation.

"The last time I was here I met a young African girl named Mawe. She was the most beautiful woman on God's green earth."

"The native rum is dangerous. It really lights a fire. It's far stronger than anything we have in our hold."

"I'm goin' to buy a bottle of rum and sit on the beach. I'll hire an African to hold an umbrella over my head. I just want to watch the Africans coming and going from the Castle to the beach for loading. That's a sight to behold."

"I've been waiting a long time for this. I make memories here that last me a lifetime. Those memories are all about whiskey, ale, brandy, rum and other things I'll not tell any of you about!"

"When I was here last, I lost an ear. That's a real story! But the scalawag that did it lost an eye for his evil deed."

Pierre continued to listen, rapidly developing an appreciation that he'd be spending his time with the captain and not these men.

Chapter 18

May 10, 1777 – Cape Coast – The Gold Coast of Guinea

TWO days earlier, Kwaku had tried to give his wife Mawusi a small glimmer of hope for finding Kisi, yet cautious not to raise her hopes unrealistically.

"It's been twenty-five days since we last saw her. The trail was dead, now maybe we've got something to follow. Already she could be far away from here. We can only trust our ancestral spirits to have kept her safe. But, a little hope is better than no hope. Now, we have something to pursue."

Ekow had a similar conversation with Ejo about Atu. Both Ekow and Kwaku at least now had clues to follow in finding their children.

It'd been two full days of travel through a formidable jungle. As they continued, the hills began to diminish and the lush jungle had turned to open ground with less trees.

It was late afternoon, with darkness approaching, when Kwaku spotted a white structure a mile or so to the east. They changed course quickly and made their way toward what they hoped would be the safe discovery of their children.

As they approached the building, they stopped to look at the ocean to the south. It was a huge expanse of water which neither had seen before. It was beyond their comprehension. If their children were on those waters, they'd be lost forever.

They began to walk faster toward the white structure not knowing what they'd find.

As they approached from the west, they slowed. Not knowing the territory or what enemy might be around, they crouched down. There was a grove of many trees nearby that stood directly behind the building, so they made their way to it.

From there they were able to see the coast line. They saw a large African village on the shoreline just east of the large white building.

Kwaku said, "We're still in Fante country so I think we'll be able to talk to the villagers. But, since we don't know anyone we should wait until first light." Ekow agreed.

~

After a fitful night, Kwaku and Ekow emerged from the trees and made their way to the village. As they entered, they received only a few curious glances from the children and adults. As they continued walking they heard a wide variety of African dialects along with some Fante.

Ekow approached a man speaking Fante to a woman. "Are you Fante and is this where you live?"

The man replied, "Yes, this is my village, but there are many different tribes living within the village, not just Fante."

"Have you always lived here?"

"Yes, this has been my home for forty years."

Pointing to the white building, Kwaku asked, "What is that place?"

"The white building belongs to the British. They've been here much longer than my forty years. But I know this village has been here much longer than they. We're Africans and they're outside visitors even though they've been here many years."

Kwaku asked, "What is this British you're speaking of? What tribe are they?"

"Oh, they're not an African tribe. They arrived by ship from another island far from here. They're white people."

"White people? What do you mean?"

The man replied, "They have white skin and we have black skin."

Kwaku and Ekow didn't understand. They had no idea anyone looked any different than themselves. On their trips north, they'd seen many different villages and tribes, but all the people they'd come across were black skinned like themselves.

"If you go to the white building you'll see the white people, but you need to be careful."

Kwaku pressed the man, "Why? What are they doing here?"

"The place is called Cape Coast Castle. It's a place where African people are brought by African traders to sell to the white men. The Africans are sent on ships to a faraway land to work."

Kwaku and Ekow slowly walked through the village. It was much larger than any they'd seen anywhere in Fante land.

Emerging from the village, they stood on the beach. As far as they could see to the right and left, they saw a rocky and sandy shore. Kwaku walked to the water, cupped his hand, captured water and scooped it into his mouth to drink. Immediately he gagged. He looked at Ekow with a look of horror.

Ekow cupped a handful of water and tried it. He gasped and spit it on the ground. Such a huge expanse of water and it couldn't be used!

Ekow looked at the harbor and saw eight large ships floating quietly. Large tree trunks were planted on each ship. Each ship had three. He wondered what the useless trees without leaves and branches were for.

As he looked to the right, he scanned the white building. The two men decided to walk toward it. Possibly there they could learn more about the fate of their children.

As they walked, a man called out to them. They turned around and saw two men sitting in the sand close to the village. They were the same two men they'd met in the jungle who'd been searching for their four tribesmen. Walking toward them, they greeted one another and sat down.

One of the Fante men said to Kwaku, "You found your way to the coast. Is it what you expected?"

"No, we had no idea. What are you learning?"

"We've discovered that a large group of two hundred men, women and children arrived here about twenty days ago. They were the last group arriving here, as no others have come since then."

The other man continued, "White men bring the Africans from the big white building down to the shore. We've not seen our tribesmen in any of the groups. We've watched many men and women being loaded on small wooden boats going out to the big ships."

The white Castle was only four hundred feet away, so Kwaku, Ekow and the two men had a clear view of all that was happening outside the building. They knew if Africans were brought from the white building to load into the small boats, they'd need to get closer to see their faces. There was no need to do that now and place themselves in danger, so the four men watched and waited.

One of the two men pointed to a ship in the harbor and said, "That ship came in last night." Pointing to another, "The small boats just finished loading Africans into that boat last night."

Immediately Kwaku and Ekow feared they may have already missed seeing their children. They also knew there was nothing to be done if Atu and Kisi were now aboard a ship.

As they watched, the ship which had recently been loaded, now had a large white canvas spread out on the bare tree at the center of the ship. Other cloths were being spread on the other two tree trunks. Soon the ship began moving away from the Cape Coast.

Kwaku and Ekow opened their pouch of dried meat and offered to share with the other two men. Their new friends had a bag of fruit and vegetables which they'd bought or traded for. The group of four men with a common mission quietly ate their meal together.

One of the men pointed seaward at the ship that had arrived the afternoon before. Men were climbing over the side to drop into one of the small boats. Africans were using sticks alongside to move the boat toward shore. As the boat drew closer, Kwaku and Ekow saw the white faces and arms of the men from the large ship. It was startling.

Fifteen men jumped from the boats onto the shore. Two of the men knelt in the sand and kissed the sandy beach while the others yelled and waved their arms. Ekow looked at Kwaku, smiled and said, "These pale men are very strange people!"

The men walked along the beach while the four Africans intently watched them. The white men had large knives in their belts. Several had a wooden object in their belts with a round iron tube sticking out from it. Was it another type of weapon?

The men were excited and jabbering in another language. Several only glanced at the four men. The men had something else on their mind as they eyed the village. They moved further down the beach and made their way into the village.

The boat which had unloaded them onto the shore had now returned to the large ship and was taking on more men. Slowly it made its way to the shore. As it unloaded, the men's behavior was the same, except for five who seemed to be more dignified.

The four Africans watched as the new group came their way. One appeared by his attire to be a chief. Another was just a boy. The young one seemed to be apprehensive yet inquisitive and stayed close to the chief.

As they passed, the boy made brief eye contact with the group of four African men and passed on. Ekow couldn't believe how white these men were!

The group disappeared into the village.

Kwaku asked, "If these white men are taking Africans by ship to other places by force, why don't they take us?"

One of the men thought and then said, "We've learned some things from the Fante in this village before you arrived. The French white men on the ships are from different tribes than the British men in the building. They're not always friends of one another, but they work together. Their goal is to find strong Africans to take to other places to work, but they need the African men in this village to load and unload the ships. They must think we're from this village.

"It isn't safe for the white men to travel inside Africa. There are dangers here which they fear. Disease, wild animals, snakes and even some tribes which would kill them. They've learned it's best to use Africans to bring other Africans to the white building. They give the African traders knives, thunder-sticks, alcohol, beads, cloth, tobacco, iron, copper and other things to bring kidnapped Africans here.

"The African traders travel far inland to many different tribes and villages. In those villages, they gather the African men who were thieves or killers. Sometimes they gather women who have been unfaithful to their husbands. If they can't find enough of those bad kinds of Africans, they find others to finish the group. I think that's why our four tribesmen and maybe your two children were taken. The traders had spent many days in collecting their quota and they were nearing the coast. They needed more people. Many people die in the trek through the jungles so sometimes they need a few more.

"Here in Africa, there are always wars among tribes and villages. Sometimes, instead of killing the enemy, they're taken as slaves. Sometimes they're sold. The Africans coming to the Castle arrive from many places for many reasons. Sometimes an evil chief in a village will even sell his own tribesmen to the African traders. It's been known to happen."

Kwaku and Ekow had difficulty accepting what they were hearing. Africans selling Africans? How could that be? They were hearing things difficult to comprehend. Their village had been so protected and they'd not heard or known these things before.

They realized this large Fante village on the shore was getting its livelihood and revenue from the slave trade. The Africans in the village entertaining the ship's crews and selling them goods seemed just as guilty as the African slave traders in the jungles.

Kwaku and Ekow were ashamed to think that Africans might be assisting the slave trade.

Chapter 19

May 11, 1777 – Cape Coast – The Gold Coast of Guinea

WHEN the moment had come for him to drop over the gunwale of the *L'ange D'or*, Pierre had hesitated. A push from the third mate took his decision away. He grabbed the heavy, bristled rope and held on as if his life depended on it. He got a glimpse of the swirling Atlantic and wooden boat twenty-five feet below him.

He lowered himself one rope rung at a time, until his feet were inside the boat. The lurching of the boat caused him to fall heavily to the bottom of the boat. He sat and waited for the rest of the men to fill it. The African men started rowing the boat to the shoreline. The surf pushed them steadily ahead into the crashing breakers. Then he heard the crunch of sand under the boat. He climbed out with his shipmates.

The surgeon, first and third mate stayed together with Pierre and the captain. The second mate had stayed aboard the *L'ange D'or* to keep it secure. They began slowly walking along the shoreline to the African village.

Pierre filled his eyes with whatever passed in front of them. The Africans were busy taking care of their daily duties and didn't seem to notice the white men among them. Pierre made eye contact with an African man sitting with three others along the shore. The man maintained eye contact until Pierre looked away. The intensity in the African's eyes made Pierre feel guilty of something.

The captain and his men moved away from the beach and into the village. Near the middle of the huts, they came to a large tent that seemed out of place. There were tables and chairs scattered around. A long wooden table held liquor which was being sold.

A number of men from the *L'ange D'or* were already seated and enjoying bottles of whiskey and tankards of ale. Renard was seated among them. He kept his head down as the captain and Pierre walked past.

The captain stepped up to the table and was given a bottle of brandy. Most of the men received a bottle of whiskey as well as a tankard of ale.

Seated at a table with the captain, surgeon and two mates, Pierre felt a bit out of place without a drink. Then the captain passed the bottle to Pierre and said, "Pierre, I'd be mighty honored if you'd have a sip of my brandy."

Pierre paused for a moment, shrugged his shoulders and took a big swig. Grimacing, he pushed the bottle back to the captain.

The first mate smiled and said, "Pierre, I'd be mighty pleased if you'd have a sip of my whiskey."

Pierre knew he couldn't show favoritism, so he took a mouthful. With a gasp, he caught his breath and passed the bottle back. He knew what was coming next. Sure enough, the surgeon pushed his tankard of ale toward Pierre and said, "Pierre, you'd show me honor by partaking of this medicinal fluid with me." The group laughed and Pierre obliged the surgeon. Then it all happened again.

Pierre sat quietly on his chair. His spinning head felt like it was floating on cotton. His empty stomach was reacting to the strange alcohol. He stood to go outside the tent for air, but his feet wobbled. He nearly fell. He reached the sunlight and promptly lost the contents of his stomach into the village dirt.

Behind him he heard the *L'ange D'or* crew laughing. Suddenly the captain burst out in a song of the seas and the others joined him...

His mama sent him off by himself,
to the deep and dark blue sea...
She said as he walked out the door,
don't forget to come back to me...
He learned the ways of the sailor's life,

for a landlubber he'd never be...

Pierre didn't hear the rest of the song as he retched again and again. His head spinning, he wiped his mouth and returned to the captain's table. Along the way, the men thumped him on his back.

The captain said, "I don't think your mother would be happy with me for encouraging that to happen. Now, you have a choice to make. If you enjoyed that, there's more where it came from. If you've had your fill, then I'll get you some water or milk. What do you say?"

Pierre, grimacing at the thought of warm milk, said, "A mug of water would be just what I need."

As he sipped his water, he watched the men around him becoming more and more drunk. None of them were vomiting, but they were becoming louder and louder. The men at Pierre's table were the exception.

The captain asked Pierre if he wanted to take a walk through the village. He welcomed the chance to leave the tent.

As they walked, Pierre saw many women and children. He asked the captain where the men were. The captain replied, "The African men are busy in the small boats rowing crews to shore as well as taking other Africans to the ships. Some of the men work inside the white Castle as guards or do other jobs such as cleaning. Many work on the ships in the harbor unloading the freight. Others are taking cargo to the ships. There are many opportunities for work in this village."

"Why did you come to the village instead of going to the Cape Coast Castle?"

"Well, you'd need to understand a few hundred years of history to understand that! The Castle and this part of the shore belong to the English. There've been many conflicts, wars and battles between our two countries. Away from Europe we can get along because of the common goals of commerce, business and profits. The North American thirteen colonies have been rebelling against Great Britain's rule. French traders and troops have been working with the colonies against Britain. Of course that doesn't help the relations between Britain and France. There are rumors that France will be helping the colonies much more in the next months and year. I think the relationship between France and England is a heated powder keg waiting to blow. Who knows where and who knows when, but war is on the horizon."

He continued, "Though we're congenial to one another, the English in the Cape Coast Castle aren't anxious to spend social time with the likes of us French sailors! So, here we are in the African village. When the slave sale takes place, you can count on the fact we'll be welcomed into the Castle. They like our gold!"

Pierre asked, "What sale are you talking about?"

"Oh, that's right, this is your first trip." The captain laughed and said, "Inside that Castle right now are approximately one thousand African men and women waiting for transport to the Caribbean and America's. The African traders are continually bringing in new people from inland Africa. In a few days, there will be a sale. I'll purchase 450 or so of those people on behalf of the ship's owner to transport to Hispaniola. There are other captains here who'll be doing the same thing. Some of them are only purchasing a hundred or so. Our ship is much larger so we'll get the lion's share of the cargo. Pierre, your education has just begun."

Pierre had been listening and was surprised to see they'd arrived at the west end of the village putting the Castle directly in front of him. The Castle was quiet and foreboding. If he didn't know what was in the Castle, he'd have thought it to be beautiful and tranquil. A peaceful and pleasant piece of architecture in an otherwise wild environment. But now, he wondered what lay within. What were those thousand people experiencing?

Suddenly, two heavy wooden doors opened in the lower wall just one hundred feet in front of him. A large wooden cart with two squeaking wheels moved through the opening. Pulled by two Africans and pushed by four more, the cart made a short turn toward the shore. It stopped and two of the men quickly shut the massive castle doors. They continued maneuvering and pushing the heavy cart seaward through the sand. There were sides on the cart so Pierre couldn't see what was inside.

He and a hesitant captain walked closer to the cart. At the shoreline were several small wooden boats with their owners waiting for the approaching load. It stopped ten feet away from the first boat. Though he was still fifteen feet from the cart, Pierre could smell decaying flesh and hear the constant buzzing of flies. He nearly gagged.

A wooden gate on the back of the cart was pulled open. Standing to the side, Pierre still couldn't see what the men were unloading. Then one of the Africans reached inside and began pulling something to the edge. It dropped heavily to the sand and startled Pierre. An African woman, younger than his own mother lay distorted in the sand. She was filthy. Pierre looked at her and saw pain on a lifeless face. Her face was frozen in a perpetual grimace she'd carry into eternity. Then a man's body was dropped on top of the woman. Two children, one only six or seven-years-old dropped onto the pile.

When the cart was empty Pierre had counted four men, three women and two children on the pile, each with their own testimony of castle life forever etched on their faces. Some of the bodies had open wounds and dried blood on them.

Pierre had been horrified when the first body dropped to the sand. He was unable to move as the horror unfolded before him.

The African men retrieved buckets, dipped them in the ocean and threw the water into the cart to wash away the blood and filth left behind. The back gate was secured and the cart began rolling away, pulled and pushed by men whose faces were blank and lifeless.

An African pushed past Pierre and drug a body to his boat. Again and again it continued until all the bodies were thrown into the wooden death boat. Pierre saw a pile of rocks with attached cords laying in the bottom of the boat.

He watched as four men rowed the boat into the harbor. Pierre looked at the captain. Captain Jean said, "They'll tie the rocks to the bodies and drop them into the harbor. I know it's a hard thing to watch for a young boy. It is for me as well, but the crabs will eat well tonight."

He continued, "I wouldn't say this to anyone else, but those souls are probably more fortunate than the 450 souls we'll take to the hard work in Hispaniola."

Pierre asked, "So, why do you do this?"

The captain looked at the innocent, ideological boy. "I suppose there was a time when I asked that question too. Every trip I take, I'm more distanced from the reality of what's happening. I've heard the same thing from many other captains and crews over the years. What used to be faces and souls are now cargo and freight. What used to be a job has now become business and profit. If I don't do this, there are many more ships, captains and crews who will. It's a fact of life."

He continued, "Watch out for the nightmares. My nightmares stopped many trips ago." He paused and placed his hand on Pierre's shoulder, "Being with you on this trip has brought me face to face with who I used to be. I'm not sure that's a good thing. Possibly my nightmares will return tonight. Perhaps now you see why the crew hides in the village drinking instead of walking the beach."

As Pierre watched the small boat, he could almost hear the splash of the six-year-old boy hitting the water and dropping into the depths of the Atlantic.

Chapter 20

May 12, 1777 – Cape Coast – The Gold Coast of Guinea

EKOW and Kwaku, along with their two new friends had learned a lot about the Atlantic Slave Trade by merely watching what was happening on the shoreline. Sitting in the shadows of the Cape Coast Castle, they felt far away from their Fante villages to the north.

Yesterday, they'd watched as a cartload of corpses were loaded into a small wooden boat. They knew the Atlantic would receive the sacrifices of the dead once again. This morning the ritual was repeated. They wondered whether any of the corpses were those villagers they'd been searching for. They'd been tempted to get closer to investigate, but fear of being taken into the Castle as replacements kept them at a distance.

They watched as the white chief and boy observed the scene unfolding before their eyes. Ekow knew the boy was about the same age as his own Atu. The captain had begun walking away while the boy watched the ocean, looking into the distance. When the boy turned, he was wiping his face. Was it the heat, or a sympathetic heart for the dead?

The second cartload of corpses had been deposited on the sand and the cart was rolling up to the large wooden doors when Ekow heard a shout from the village behind him. He turned around in time to see a woman pointing to the north.

The men stood to see what she was pointing to. In the distance they could see a line of Africans leaving the forest and walking toward them. A small door on the east side of the Castle opened and five English men emerged with four Africans. They watched and waited as the line of captives drew closer.

Ekow thought the line of slaves looked like a procession of ants similar to what he'd often seen in the forest. He had once watched a procession steadily and naively crawl into the tongue range of a large anteater. Ekow thought the white Castle would soon be receiving these people into whatever lay within.

Kwaku said, "Do you think our children could be in this group just arriving?"

Ekow replied, "No. we followed their trail to the coast. They were already here when we arrived. They're either on ships heading to sea, in the Castle, or..."

He stopped talking and then said, "We'll watch and wait."

The line was getting closer. They were being led by a large African man. Walking alongside the procession were Africans guarding the large group of men and women.

Suddenly there was shouting from the line of new captives. They watched as two men broke away from the group, likely sensing freedom when they spied the village. They had wooden yokes around their necks and were bravely yet clumsily running to escape. Two white men pointed their wooden sticks and iron tubes at the Africans. There was a puff of smoke and a boom in the quietness. Then another. Both running men fell to the ground. Now, the Fante men knew about the thunder-sticks. A third guard with a sword approached the two Africans who had escaped. The sword flashed in the sunlight multiple times.

The guard held his sword in the air and waved to the horrified Africans. Casually he began walking to the captives, wiping his blade on a cloth.

When he arrived at the now motionless line of slaves, they all began moving forward once again.

Soon, the line rounded the rear corner of the Castle and came to the open door. They began filing into the dark doorway one at a time. The four men watched the scene before them. The faces of the newly arrived Africans were full of sadness and terror. Fear of the unknown was obviously being felt by everyone in the group. The two hundred men and women disappeared into the Castle and the door clanked shut with a metallic and secure clang. Everything was deathly quiet.

Ekow looked to the north in time to see several large and hungry vultures landing near the two escaped men. This would not be their first feast. Possibly those two men were the fortunate ones.

~

Kisi, unknowingly, was only several hundred feet west of Kwaku, Ekow and the other two men. She listened to the now familiar shuffle of more people coming down the hallway descending into the dungeon depths of Cape Coast Castle. The guards carrying torches came first with women following. The flickering flames cast an unnerving light on the faces of these new African slaves. As Kisi looked at the faces of her own group, she saw the same eerie light. The difference was stark. Those just entering looked reasonably healthy. Her group looked haggard, hurt and abused.

Kisi felt a wave of guilt as a thought came to her mind. *'The freshness of these new African women will be more attractive to the white men above.'*

Then she felt guilty for hoping her own group would be ignored. The women continued filing past. Their new home lay further into the Castle depths.

Soon, another set of torches lit the way for a large group of men shuffling into their new home. Some of the men were the age of Atu. Some were as old as her own father.

That thought immediately troubled her as she thought of her father, mother and others in her village. What were they thinking? It'd been twenty-seven days since she and Atu had been taken captive. Had the villagers given up their search? Then she thought of her father and knew that wouldn't be true. She knew he wouldn't tire in his efforts to find her. She thought Ekow would be the same in trying to find his son.

It was obvious to her that the Castle was a fortress. She knew her father wasn't a warrior. He'd been a hunter and a man of the soil all his life. There had been times he'd picked up his bow, arrows and spear to deal with intruding raiders, but that wasn't his nature. What could these native men do in dealing with the well supplied white men who obviously were well trained in controlling others? There wasn't anything to do but wait and see what was to come.

Kisi had been thankful she hadn't been selected for a trip to the white men's rooms. There were many white men above who had apparently lived on this remote shoreline without their wives and families, otherwise they wouldn't be so quick to take advantage of African women.

She wondered how long she and her group would be captive in this place. Obviously, they were getting weaker every day. Their future usefulness was fading. Women in her group had already died. Those living didn't wait for the guards to find the dead. Instead they'd pull the corpses into the dungeon hallway to be found by the guards. The stench never left their nostrils. When one or two corpses would be pulled away, there were more to be found.

How long would this hell-hole last?

~

A hundred feet away and ten feet lower, Atu waited. That's all there was to do. More men were arriving which made their chamber even fuller. The new men were stronger than those who had been here for weeks so it was more difficult to keep his space against the wall.

There were times when fighting broke out among the prisoners. Periodically someone would lose their mind and use his chain to strangle or hit someone. When the fighting started, others nearby would join in to defend themselves. The noise would bring the guards running with their torches to find the troublemakers. They'd be taken out of the group and up the hall. To where? For what? Who knew?

Sometimes the entire group would be chained to iron links fastened in the walls. If someone was chained near the floor, they could sit or lay. Since the floor was covered with vomit, urine and feces, that certainly wasn't the ideal place. If they were chained higher on the wall, they had no choice but to stand. Sometimes the chaining lasted for days. To rest, a prisoner had to hang from the chain which was very painful. Sometimes Atu wondered if the guards had forgotten them.

The time drug on and on. It'd been twenty-seven days since they'd been kidnapped. How long could they continue?

Atu wondered about Kisi. He hadn't seen her. He knew she was young and strong but this torment took so much from even the toughest among them. He'd already seen many corpses and wondered how many more there would be. Would he and Kisi survive this hell?

Chapter 21

May 12, 1777 – Les Cayes, Saint-Domingue (now Haiti), Island of Hispaniola

FRANCOIS leaned against the large mahogany tree and rested. His long legs stretched out before him and his red hair flowed in the Caribbean breeze. Fanning himself with a banana tree leaf, he nestled the rum bottle between his legs. The sun had been merciless that morning and was only getting stronger as the day wore on.

He thought about his wife and boys at their plantation home likely enjoying a cool breeze and hearty lunch. He hoped they thought about his labors on the plain and what he endured to bring them some degree of comfort.

Though this land of Saint-Domingue, occupying the western one-third of the island of Hispaniola was incredibly beautiful, the heat, humidity and incessant bugs were troublesome for someone of his position. Sometimes he felt sorry for himself, but in reality his life was good. Seven days a week it was his responsibility to maintain profitability on the Labreche plantation. He was thankful for other men who managed in his absence so he could have days off with his family.

Francois had twenty-five French overseers who managed the absentee-owner's one-thousand African workers and made sure production happened with efficiency. Each of the overseers had multiple French helpers who took care of the slave labor, kept them from escaping and administered discipline.

Francois' top overseer was Sylvain. The two had grown up in northern France in a small farming village. Together they'd attended school, worked side-by-side in Sylvain's father's fields and had become close friends.

They'd married within a year of one another and each had two children. Francois had two boys and Sylvain, two girls. The men were thirty-four-years-old and had brought their families to this small town of Les Cayes in southwestern Saint-Domingue seven years earlier.

The area of Les Cayes was extraordinarily beautiful. The mountains stretching beyond the coastal lowland plains went on forever, or so it seemed. There were magnificent beaches, waterfalls, rivers and streams. The wildlife was bountiful. Fish, deer, birds and ducks were plentiful.

The ground was so fertile, it was said, that a farmer could throw a seed over his shoulder and it'd begin sprouting that same day. Francois knew better, but the ground was truly more fertile than his native France.

The tobacco had the largest leaves anywhere and made it a great commodity to ship to Europe.

Indigo for the manufacturing of royal blue ink to be used as dye was a much sought after product in the textile mills of England and Europe.

Cotton had been grown in Saint-Domingue for centuries. The mountains produced coffee beans which supplied a growing market for the return leg of the Atlantic Trade Triangle.

Sugarcane grew well and was a huge profit maker for the Les Cayes region in its production of rum and raw sugar.

All these products required large amounts of labor to plant, till, harvest and process. Francois knew he was doing an excellent job in managing the plantation for the Labreche family owners who lived in France. He thought, with pride, about all the production around him as he sipped rum under his mahogany tree. He smiled as he thought of this tree being his mahogany office. He knew many people in Europe had their furniture made from the type of wood he was leaning against.

Hearing a noise behind him, he stood quickly and cursed himself as his bottle of rum tipped and spilled into the ground. Sylvain was riding toward him on his bay mare and laughed as he saw the rum bottle laying on its side. "What's the matter my friend? Did you have too much to drink?"

Francois couldn't help but smile at his bald friend. They'd been through a lot together in their work in Saint-Domingue. Their families lived on the main grounds of the plantation. They literally had all they needed to survive and then some. Life was good and neither family desired the sophisticated life of Paris. This place was their home.

"Francois, I thought you needed to know. I had some trouble at the sugarcane mill this morning. There was an accident, but we dealt with it."

"What happened?"

"A worker named Billy was pushing sugarcane into the stone trough and wheel for squeezing. He slipped in the water that was feeding into the wheel and had his arm crushed. Our overseer used a machete to remove the arm and then stopped the bleeding with a firebrand. Billy died anyway."

Francois cursed, "Don't these ignorant Africans know what happens to our profits when they're not careful? That accident leaves us short-handed!"

Then they both laughed at the joke he'd just made as they thought of the African who'd just lost his arm. "Ha, short-handed. That was funny, wasn't it?"

Francois continued, "Did you do the usual?"

"Yeah, I tied the severed arm to a wooden pole next to the wheel. The other Africans will see it."

"Thanks Sylvain. We're never done teaching them, are we? Every African we lose through their stupidity is a huge loss. It's one thing to lose someone to sickness, but stupidity is inexcusable. After all, it's another three months before we get our next supply of blacks from Africa. With the losses we have from accidents, runaways and disease, it's difficult to have enough people to get all the work done."

Sylvain galloped off to supervise the overseers who were managing the 1,000 field hands on their 2,500 acres. Things were going well in spite of the daily issues, which were highly annoying.

Francois walked to another tree where his horse was tied and patted his white stallion on the neck. Stepping into the stirrup he swung his leg over the saddle. Settling in, he walked him onto the plain. He loved admiring the four square miles of plantation property. They took great care in managing the various products in each of those miles. Looking north to the mountains, the plain before him was green and lush with tobacco. Looking east he admired the tall green crop of sugarcane. To the west was another stand of sugar cane. As he walked his horse, he turned south to see a square mile of cotton. Other crops would be rotated periodically, but for now, the top crops were the tobacco, cotton and sugarcane.

As he headed south toward the coast which was only four miles away he made a mental note to take his family to the beach on Sunday. He nudged the stallion into a gallop and headed toward his home and family.

Chapter 22

PIERRE counted the lines he'd marked on the paper tacked to the wall of his berth. It'd been thirty-one days since he'd last seen his mother. That meant another five months before seeing her again. He missed her. He realized she'd had no choice in sending him as an indentured servant with the captain. If he were to have any future at all, he'd need to finish his education. But if they had no place to live, he'd need to work and thus have no education. The captain had said he'd pay for the next six month debt on the cottage if he'd take the voyage. That didn't do anything for the six months after that. The path forward for his mother seemed difficult. But, as he watched the lives of the sailors, that of the village Africans and certainly that of the enslaved Africans, he was feeling fortunate. He'd need to let fate plot his course and destiny.

They'd been in port at Cape Coast six days which meant today was the day for the slave sale. They'd been busy loading their *L'ange D'or* cargo on board the small boats and had sold most of the goods to the village Africans and Englishmen. The remaining cargo went to other ship's crews.

After the ship's cargo was unloaded, the crew began loading new supplies and goods for their voyage to Hispaniola. The voyage from Cape Coast to Saint-Domingue would take approximately three months, so a huge store of food and fresh water needed to be loaded for the 450 slaves and forty-two crew.

They finished the task of loading the ship. The men then readied the lower decks for the soon-to-be arriving African cargo of black gold.

Pierre assisted in attaching rigged chains to eyelets impaled in the posts, floors and walls of the second and third decks of the ship. There were secondary decks under the forecastle and stern ends of the ship for additional slaves. The main deck was the working top deck of the ship. Below that was the second deck usually used to store non-human cargo but on this slaver, the deck would be entirely used for Africans. The third deck was used for Africans as well as cargo. On the sidewalls of both the second and third deck were shelves where additional slaves were kept. The bottom or fourth deck was used for boxes and barrels of freight.

In the areas beneath the forecastle and stern, Pierre was shocked to see there was only thirty inches of space from the top to bottom for those Africans lying on the hard, wooden shelves. Other slaves would be packed like cordwood on the wooden floors and shackled to the iron rings secured to the ship.

On the second deck, the men would be at the bow end, boys were mid-ship and the women and girls were at the stern. Most laid with their heads on starboard or on port side. In the very center of the ship where room permitted, they'd lay bow to stern.

The third deck would be only men. The captain had said, "The majority of Africans we buy will be male. Enough females will be bought to enable breeding on the island to reproduce future slaves."

Pierre had responded, "Captain, I've heard you use words like cargo when you talked about Africans. Now you said they'd breed. That sounds like you're talking about animals, not humans."

"I guess when you've been at this as long as I have, it's easy to start thinking of them in that way. It's not right, I know, but it is what it is and that's how Europeans and Englishmen think of the Africans."

The calculated space allotted to each adult male was six feet long by one and one-half foot wide. The women had slightly less and the children even less. Pierre was amazed at the efficient use of space aboard the ship. He couldn't imagine what it'd be like to see such a mass of humanity in the holds.

He'd asked the captain, "Why do you chain the slaves? They can't go anywhere since they're on board the ship. It's not like they could escape."

Captain Jean said, "I could tell you many stories. Since the crew is outnumbered ten to one, the last thing we'd want is a mutiny with the slaves taking over the ship. Secondly, when slaves are brought to the main deck for washing or exercise, they've been known to jump from the ship into the ocean. They think losing their life would be better than the unknown of where they're going."

He continued, "I heard about a Portuguese ship where the slaves overtook the crew. The crew was killed and the slaves then had a ship on the open ocean. They had no idea how to navigate, manage the sails or how to get where they were going. Eventually they starved on the open seas. Later an English cargo ship found it adrift. It'd become a ghost ship with everyone dead."

The *L'ange D'or* crew had spent some of their leave time on shore drinking and carousing. Last evening, when it'd been time to return to the ship, two men were missing, one of them Renard. At six o'clock this morning, the captain had sent the second mate to shore with four other crewmen to find the missing men.

The captain told Pierre, "It's not uncommon for crewmen to walk away from their ship and never return. Sometimes they fall into a bad situation on shore and are never seen again. Perhaps they take advantage of an African's wife and then the husband takes matters into his own hands. We don't know what's happened to Renard and his friend, but maybe we'll find out."

The captain, surgeon and first mate would be going ashore at seven o'clock to start the process of purchasing slaves. The captain asked Pierre if he wanted to join him. Pierre hesitated and then said, "Sure, might as well."

As the captain and his assistants readied to go ashore, the second mate and the four men arrived back on board the *L'ange D'or*. Renard and his friend were not with them.

The mate said to the captain, "When we arrived on shore we began asking as to the whereabouts of our two crewmen. Believe me, if two white men stayed on shore overnight, some in the village would know. The villagers know a white man shouldn't be overnight in their village. No one was sharing any information so I began spreading some money around. Soon enough we were taken to the crewmen's location. Beyond the eastern side of the village was a place where garbage is thrown for the animals and vultures. On the pile were Renard and his friend. Both of them had slit throats. I think we know Renard well enough to know he'd created some trouble someone couldn't tolerate. We'll be missing two crewmen for the middle passage to the island."

That was the only time Pierre heard the captain curse. Losing two crewmen was a very major problem and the captain knew it'd create more work for the rest of the crew. The captain thanked the first mate and his men for their efforts.

Pierre felt a twinge of pleasure when he heard about Renard's death. That also brought a twinge of guilt. He involuntarily touched his throat as he thought about what Renard and his friend had gone through.

There had been something twisted about Renard that Pierre couldn't trust. Though the whipping of Renard had happened, Pierre had still feared there would be yet another bad encounter with the man. Now, that was a worry he could put aside.

The captain, surgeon, first mate and Pierre clambered over the side, descended the rope ladder and entered the boat that had just brought the search party back to the ship.

Soon they were ashore. The captain, promptly at seven o'clock began walking to a door of the Castle which opened before he arrived.

There were obviously sentries or guards inside who watched everything happening on the outside.

As Pierre walked through the door, he entered a hallway. At the end, it opened into a green courtyard. He stopped and looked around. He looked up at the Castle and saw multiple levels.

There was the large building in the middle of the courtyard, as well as smaller huts along the inside wall, likely for the workers. He noticed many white men who were probably Englishmen. Several African men and women were also busy with their work.

The white building wasn't the only magnificent thing on this shoreline. He was struck by the beauty of the lush greenery and flowers within the courtyard.

The captain and his small crew headed to a large building. A very official looking white man emerged from a doorway. He and the captain shook hands and spoke together in a language Pierre didn't understand. He assumed it was English. It was an inspiring moment for Pierre as he learned of yet another of the captain's abilities.

Captain Jean introduced the English Governor of the Cape Coast Castle to his crew. They entered a large room with desks and chairs. The governor introduced his clerk to the captain. The governor left and the captain sat at a desk. The clerk returned with a pile of papers which the captain began reading. On a blank piece of paper he periodically wrote down some numbers.

The captain told his crew, "There are a thousand men, women and children here at the Castle. I'm looking through the roster which indicates their gender, approximate age, general health and how long they've been here.

"The English have already paid the African slave traders for the people, so we'll be purchasing directly from the English. I'm searching for the Africans I think would best serve the plantation managers in Saint-Domingue. The sale will begin at high noon."

He continued looking through the rosters and writing down numbers. It'd take a while.

Pierre walked back into the courtyard and sat on a shaded bench. A black woman in a white dress came to him and spoke in a language he didn't understand. She tried again in another. He still didn't understand, then she said in beautiful French, *"Puis-je vous apporter de l'eau?"*

Pierre's mouth dropped open and he said, *"Oui madame, oui, oui!"*

The woman walked away. He couldn't believe it! She'd asked him very politely and formally if he'd like to have some water. How could it be that an ignorant, heathen, uncivilized African woman would know his language? She'd tried two other languages with Pierre before French. Counting her own African language, that would be four!

She arrived with a glass of water, curtsied and handed it to him. She smiled and he thanked her. She turned and walked away.

He couldn't wait to tell his mother about his education. Every day he was learning so much about things he'd never have learned in Bordeaux.

The captain emerged from the office with the surgeon and first mate. Pierre put the cup on the ground and joined the group as they headed to the door leading outward to the shore.

Once outside, the captain told the men, "I've identified the potential men and women I hope to purchase. We'll return at noon. Several other captains will be going through the rosters as well. Then we'll begin the bidding process for our 450 men and women."

As the crew walked to the shore to catch a small boat to their ship, Pierre noticed the same four African men sitting nearby. They were watching the captain's group intently. Again, he locked eyes with one of the men who seemed to look right into his very soul.

A Portuguese captain with two men passed them on the beach. The captains smiled at one another and saluted. As Pierre turned and watched, the men entered the door from which the *L'ange D'or* crew had just exited. It looked like the competition had arrived.

Chapter 23

ATU began yet another day of captivity sitting in a few inches of vomit and filth. Standing, he tried to shake off the excess as he leaned against the wall. Counting the days in the Castle, it'd now been thirty days since Kisi and he had been abducted.

As always, his mind turned toward her. He couldn't believe how quickly fate had brought Kisi into his life and just as quickly took her away. Second on his mind were his parents and his Fante village. What were they thinking and doing about the sudden disappearance of both of them? Would they think wild animals had killed them? Did they think they'd run off? Neither option would make any sense.

If they couldn't find a logical reason for the loss of Atu and Kisi, would they have considered the possibility of them being taken captive? Following a trail wouldn't normally be too difficult for villagers who spent their life in a jungle. However, with rain, the jungle ferns and undergrowth would quickly spring back to life. Even if the villagers found their way to the shoreline, how could they liberate them from such a secure fortress?

Atu was rapidly losing hope for any kind of rescue. He wondered what would be next. As the days slowly passed, he was continually hoping something would change. Anything would be better than this horrendous dungeon.

As he thought about his plight, a light flickered on the wall as someone descended the dungeon hallway. Soon, ten large and muscular African men rounded the corner and stopped. They were careful not to step into the deeper end of the dungeon where this group of men were located.

The captives began following two of the guards out of the dungeon. Each captive put his hands on the shoulders of the man in front of him. The guards had whips and didn't hesitate lashing anyone who dropped their arms. The procession slowly walked upward. They passed several chambers where women and children were located. Atu looked ahead and saw a flicker of bright sunlight beckoning them forward. There was a doorway leaking sunlight into the depths of the Cape Coast Castle.

As he got closer to the doorway he wondered what lay ahead. Was his time in the dungeon finally coming to an end? His turn came and he was almost blinded by the bright sunlight. As his eyes adjusted, the line stopped. He looked up and saw the sun in the eastern sky. In his village he knew in another hour or two his friends and family would soon begin the largest meal of their day at noon.

Lowering his head, he saw the courtyard filled with hundreds of African men, women and children. He heard a woman call a man's name. Immediately he heard the crack of a whip and the scream of the woman. He knew no one else would be calling out to their husband or father.

He looked for Kisi but couldn't see her anywhere in the mass of black and filthy humanity. The captives were naked and under the scrutiny of the guards. Large wooden barrels of water and many buckets were situated around the courtyard. The guards began pushing individual men or women toward the buckets and barrels. Each person was given a small sliver of time to wash the dungeon filth from their bodies.

Soon there were many glistening black bodies standing in lines around the yard. Some faces only subtly hinted at the humiliation of nakedness, the past abuse and the sadness of being far from home. Others showed the lines of tragedy. Still others had a rage and anger barely contained under the surface. Atu was feeling all of those emotions but knew he had to be in control if he wanted to survive.

It was sad to see the once proud, self-sufficient and wonderfully peaceful African villagers now degraded to something less than animals. Atu felt his eyes filling with tears.

At the far end of the courtyard a wooden platform had been erected. The men and women stood quietly in the hot sunshine, waiting. Waiting for the unknown and whatever would be next.

Suddenly, an African man broke away from the line of men he was standing in and began running to the staircase leading up to the white building's balcony. Two guards immediately ran after him. Though the African was weakened by his captivity, he ran amazingly fast. The lines of Africans watched as he ascended the first and second set of stairs and then another. He stood on the fourth floor balcony, surveying the courtyard below. He was obviously weighing his options as the armed African guards arrived at each end of his balcony.

The brave African captive had just experienced freedom if but for a minute. Again, he looked down at the men and women in line. He clenched his fists in the air and yelled something in an African dialect which Atu didn't understand. The man's proud statement however was definitely one of defiance. He climbed the rail overlooking the courtyard and jumped. There was an involuntary groan from the African men and women as they all heard the man hit the stone courtyard beneath. He screamed as bones broke.

The English guards ran quickly to the scene. Bones were sticking through the skin of one of the African's legs. An Englishman said to the guards, "He's of no use to anyone now. Finish him."

Though their English language was unknown to all the Africans watching, it was easy to see what was happening.

The guards reached down and grabbed the man by each arm and began dragging him away to a door. The Englishman-in-charge yelled, "No! Take him to the middle of the courtyard."

The guards obeyed and dropped him in the center. He told a guard to sever the African's head. One of the guards pulled his sword from its scabbard with no hesitation and with one flash of the blade, the man's head dropped to the ground. The guards and Englishmen walked away knowing they didn't need to explain anything to the African men and women who had just watched in horror. The body and head remained behind as a reminder to the Africans of the results of rebellion. In Atu's mind, the mutilated body was a badge of honor and strength. The man's courage stirred Atu deeply and Atu knew he wasn't alone. The Englishmen had just made a huge mistake. Whatever the Englishmen had taken from the Africans, it had just been replenished.

One of the clerks said, "Governor, the men and women have all been cleaned. Seven ship's captains have been through the rosters and are ready for the sale. They've been instructed to be here at high noon."

"I presume all the African traders have been compensated for the men and women they've brought to us? The Africans are now legally all English property?"

"Yes, that's all been taken care of. They're all paid."

Licking his thick lips and rubbing his white, soft hands together the English Governor thanked the clerk. He pulled a watch from his vest pocket and looked up at the sun and said, "In fifteen minutes ring the chapel bell."

Chapter 24

May 15, 1777 – Cape Coast Castle – The Gold Coast of Guinea

EKOW and Kwaku had been at the Cape Coast port for four days. They sat on shore just west of the Fante village and a stone's throw away from the Cape Coast Castle.

They, along with the two men they'd met near their home village, desperately wanted to be doing something. Anything other than sitting on this hot beach waiting. Waiting. Waiting for something to happen.

They'd thought about leaving this area and exploring east or west along the coastline looking for Kisi and Atu. But, they knew it'd be like trying to find a tiny lizard somewhere in the ferns of their jungle. Staying here would be their best chance. This was where all the ships were.

Over the last four days, they'd seen a lot of activity. Ships were coming and going. Wooden transport boats were constantly moving between the shore and large ships with cargo. Corpses were leaving the Castle for burial at sea. With all the African bodies being transported to the watery depths, they wondered how many more Africans could be housed in the Castle.

This morning they'd watched as activities at the Castle seemed to be increasing. Important looking men from the ships had come ashore and disappeared into the white building. Then they'd left and another group took their place. It happened several times.

Ekow and Kwaku had talked together of options. They'd spoken to many Fante in the village about what was happening at the harbor and in the Castle. Every time they pondered the situation, they came to the same conclusion. The only place their son and daughter could be was in the white building, already on a ship out at sea, or no longer living.

Sadly, with a patience born of desperation, they continued their vigil by the ocean.

The sun was directly overhead and the day was hot and sultry. Just then a loud noise came from the Castle tower. All eyes turned upward. The repetitive clanging of the bell continued.

They saw several boats leaving the shore and heading for the ships in the harbor. Watching, they saw men climbing over the side of their ships and beginning their shoreward jaunt.

Shortly, the boats beached and important looking men came ashore with their men. They made an impressive delegation as the group of thirty or so sailors walked toward the Castle. The door opened and the line of men disappeared inside.

~

Pierre expected the same courtyard scene as he'd experienced earlier that morning. But as he, the captain, surgeon and first mate entered the grassy area surrounded by the white building, he was astounded to see hundreds of African men and women standing in orderly rows.

English and African guards with flintlock pistols, muskets and swords were strategically placed throughout the courtyard. It was obvious they were in control. Other men carried short whips and walked among the groups of Africans.

The clanging of the bell stopped. Then, there was utter quiet. The Governor stood on the platform and with a booming voice said, "Welcome to Cape Coast Castle. Captains, please sit in the chairs in front of the auction block with your assistants."

Seven captains with their men walked in front of the wooden platform and took their places. Pierre felt incredibly out of place, but sat in a chair beside Captain Jean.

The governor said, "We have one thousand African men and women in the courtyard today. Additional groups of people are on their way here from the north with the African traders and will begin arriving at the coast in one week. It's important we get as much of this property sold today as possible to make room for more. More ships will be arriving in the next few days."

Captain Jean opened a large journal, as did the other captains. He knew exactly how many men and women he needed to purchase. He wasn't interested in any young children but would readily buy children who were over the age of twelve-years-old, if they were healthy and strong.

An English guard with a whip brought the first African man to the platform. The African's eyes were frantic and darting from the right to the left. It was obvious, if he would've had anywhere to go, he would've ran. But he didn't have any options other than going up the steps to the platform.

The man was in his twenties, tall and muscular. A forged iron band of steel was secured around his neck. There was a loop of iron on the shackle and a four foot length of wrought iron chain was hanging in front of him.

All seven doctors stepped up to the man, quickly walked around him, squeezed his arms and thighs, opened his mouth, inspected his teeth, and looked at his feet and eyes. The doctors spoke to their captains and the bidding for the first man began. A second man was brought to the platform to be examined by the doctors while the first man was being sold. Quickly the first sale was completed and a tag was tied to his chain. The African was escorted off the platform to begin a new line. The cycle continued efficiently.

A young woman was brought to the platform. She, like the others before her, looked much like a frantic baby rabbit. Pierre was riveted by what was happening, yet feeling miserable for what the Africans were going through. The woman had no neck shackle but wore one around her wrist. A shorter chain was dangling from her wrist shackle and was resting lazily on the ground. Again, the inspection. Probing, squeezing, poking and examining. Quickly the bidding began and soon came to an end. She left the platform and rapidly another male moved into the selling position.

The captain kept accurate records of each male and female. He was successful in his bids most of the time. He knew he needed to attain his quota as soon as possible. He didn't want to be in a position of buying late and potentially owning weaker, less healthy and smaller men or women.

The afternoon drug on and on. Occasionally, African women working for the governor arrived with large glasses of water and platters of fruit for the captains and crewmen. Pierre couldn't help but feel ashamed as he drank and ate in front of the Africans. He couldn't imagine how they felt. They had to be hungry and dehydrated standing so long in the hot sun. As if reading Pierre's mind, the captain said, "These Africans live in the sun. They probably come from the desert and are accustomed to little water and lots of sun. That's the reason their skin is so black. They're doing fine."

~

Kisi was feeling faint. The hot sun was having no mercy. It was almost as merciless as the men drinking their water and eating their fruit in front of them. Some of the men and women had been so terrified, the guard had to use his whip to move them to the platform. She watched as the guard came nearer and nearer her position.

Her heart started beating faster and faster and then it was her turn. She knew there would be a thousand pairs of eyes watching her. She also knew one of those pairs would be Atu's. She'd been scanning the groups of men to catch a glimpse of him, but with no success.

Then the guard with the whip looked in her eyes, nearly daring her to defy him. She quickly stepped forward. With her head held high, she climbed the platform with a confidence and pride much greater than what she felt. Her heart was beating so fast it felt like it'd jump from her chest.

She stood quietly in front of the men. They probed, pushed and squeezed her just as she'd seen them do to all the others. She nearly cried out in humiliation and fear. She felt like an animal being inspected for slaughter. Finally it was over and the bidding began, then ended. An important man with a boy by his side smiled at his purchase.

~

Atu watched with growing anger and rage as Kisi went through the process. He'd started to understand what was happening. At the beginning it seemed like an inspection. As time went on he could see this for what it was. This was an acquisition of property.

Then it was Atu's turn to go to the platform. Kisi was just twenty feet away from him in the line. They made eye contact as he strode to the platform steps. He kept his eyes on her, as she did on him. He couldn't believe they weren't married. He saw tears glistening on her face. He hoped she wouldn't cry out, because he knew he'd not be able to stand idle if she were whipped.

Then, the bidding began. There were words he didn't understand. Then the man on the platform pointed to an important man from one of the ships. The man smiled and leaned over to the boy beside him and said something. The boy smiled and made eye contact with Atu who looked to be the same age as himself.

~

Pierre was growing tired as the day wore on. Finally, the governor stood and stopped the process. He said, "Tomorrow's another day. We'll begin at seven o'clock and run the sale until we're done."

The Africans were escorted by the guards to a doorway in the white building to return to their dungeons. The captains and crews left by a different door to the beach, a waiting boat and substantial meals aboard their ships.

At dinner in the captain's quarters, as Pierre served them their meal, the captain said, "Thanks to each of you for your part in today's success. We were able to purchase 220 men and 80 women. Tomorrow we'll try to purchase another 150 men to fill our quota of 450. It's been a hot and difficult day, but successful. I'm thankful for this land of Africa and the bountiful harvest she's yielded to us. I think the plantation owners in Hispaniola will be very happy."

In the morning, the group again heard the bell toll and they made their way ashore for another day of purchasing. The captain filled his quota at three o'clock in the afternoon. He and his small crew went to the Castle office to settle the tally and make payment. The captain and clerk went over their records to reconcile the two tallies. Then, the captain paid the English clerk in gold to seal the sale and gathered the receipt. The property had now become his cargo.

As they headed to the boat, the captain said, "Tomorrow we'll begin loading the food, water, kegs, crates and other cargo. In a few days we'll bring the Africans aboard and get them secured below deck. We hope to raise anchor and sail in four or five days."

Chapter 25

May 19, 1777 – Cape Coast – The Gold Coast of Guinea

EKOW and Kwaku had watched four days earlier as the ship's crews made multiple trips into and out of the Castle. Then, beginning two days ago, they began watching intently as Africans were brought out of the white building and loaded on the small boats. They looked carefully at each black face that walked the shoreline to the waiting boats. The many sad faces were frozen in fear as they filed past and made their short journey to the large ships.

There had been no sign of Ekow's son Atu or Kwaku's daughter Kisi. As the approaching darkness began pushing the western hot sun out of yet another day, the procession of slaves to the boats diminished and then stopped.

The fathers had another fitful night. They still had no clue as to the whereabouts of their children.

Another beautiful sunrise gradually imposed itself into another African day. They watched as a ship hoisted the white square canvas up a bare tree trunk on one of the ships in the harbor. The clanking of heavy iron chains rattled across the bay. Shortly the ship moved away from the coastline. Gradually becoming smaller, it became a dot on the horizon and then disappeared entirely from their view.

There was the now familiar scraping of iron against iron as a door opened in the white wall of the Castle. Again, the single file line of African slaves proceeded toward the beach.

The fathers drew closer and looked desperately for a familiar face. The faces of the men, women and children marching past were filled with fear and sadness. They kept their faces down. Was it shame that kept their eyes downward, or was it fear of the armed men steering them toward the boats?

Suddenly Kwaku gasped as he saw Kisi moving toward them. Ekow looked to see what had prompted his sudden expression. Kwaku pointed at Kisi. She was a hollow shell of what she'd been when they'd last seen her in their village. That seemed so long ago when she and Atu had taken their fateful walk into the rain forest jungle.

Her eyes were looking at the sand below her and the feet of the person in front of her. There was an iron wrist band with a chain dangling from one of her arms.

Kwaku, without thinking yelled, "Kisi! Kisi!"

Startled, she looked up with hope as she heard her father's voice. Could it actually be him? Kisi responded with a loud voice, "Father!"

Their eyes met for a moment until an African guard with a whip lashed Kisi on her bare back. Almost as quickly another guard ran to Kwaku and struck him violently across the face with his whip. Blood immediately appeared on his cut cheek.

Helplessly, Kwaku and Ekow watched as Kisi shuffled past and approached a boat. A guard pushed her into the water and over the gunwale into the waiting boat. She disappeared in the group of twenty other Africans. The boat was pushed into the waves and then, Kwaku saw her again. Their eyes locked as the boat was rapidly oared toward a large ship. Then it was over. She was gone!

With blood streaming down his face, Kwaku looked at Ekow and wept.

They renewed their vigil for a hopeful glimpse of Atu. The stream of Africans filing past was almost impossible to comprehend. Why would these white people enslave so many Africans? Then they remembered that other Africans were also involved in the enslavement of their black neighbors.

~

Atu had watched as Kisi was placed in a line of women in the courtyard. The women were marched out of the Castle. Two hours later, a guard roughly shoved Atu into a line of men. As the African men stood upright with their heads held high, a guard came behind them and struck the backs of their heads to force them down. One African man continued to hold his head high. He was pulled from the line and whipped multiple times. Then he was pushed back into line. The African wisely kept his head down, as did Atu and the others.

As they began shuffling across the courtyard, Atu was getting nearer and nearer to the large door. His turn was coming for whatever lay ahead. He emerged onto a sandy beach he'd seen weeks before.

He looked up to see many wooden boats on the shoreline and some, loaded with Africans, were already in the bay. Noticing the large ships in the harbor, he now knew what was ahead. They were leaving Africa, his home.

In that brief glance upward, he saw four African men sitting in the sand twenty feet away.

~

It was at that moment Ekow saw his son. Atu had once been a proud, upright, strong and handsome young man. Ekow was now witness to what weeks in captivity had done to his boy. Just as with Kisi, his son had become thin and weak. The son before him had shoulders that were sagging, arms listless by his side, head hanging and a large iron collar around his neck.

Ekow wanted desperately to cross the twenty feet of sand and wrap his arms around his son. He knew that would be a death wish. But the father-heart in him overpowered caution and he yelled, "Atu!"

Atu looked up just in time to see a white guard strike his father with the butt handle of his whip. He immediately saw the gash fill with blood on his father's forehead. Blood began dripping into his eyes and down his cheeks as their eyes met.

Atu mouthed the word, *'Father'* across the distance as their eyes met. He continued his slow shuffle to the boat. He saw the horrible agony on his father's face and knew it wasn't from the whip.

To fight or flee would be futile. To stay in Africa would mean a quick death for him and most likely his father. To stay would mean losing sight of his fiancé Kisi who he knew was already aboard one of the several ships in the harbor. He had no idea which one she'd boarded. He only knew she'd been taken two hours earlier through the *'Door of No Return'*.

~

Pierre stood on the starboard side of the main deck and watched as the boats loaded with Africans approached the ship. Over the last two days, the ship had taken on the crates, kegs and other products necessary for three months of sailing to Hispaniola. Now it was time for the live cargo.

As the boats approached the ship, ropes kept them close for the loading of the 'Black Gold'. A large web of heavy ropes was hanging over the side of the *L'ange D'or* upon which the Africans desperately clung, as they began climbing aboard.

Pierre watched the emotions of those setting foot on deck. Their faces were full of fear and horror. The unknown of what was ahead, as well as the atrocities the people had already endured had touched these Africans deeply, and were now touching him.

In contrast, as he watched the faces of the captain, surgeon and mates, he saw blank faces. They showed no emotion. He wondered how many times someone needed to experience this scene to get to a place of apathy.

The Africans were quickly steered below-deck to their new homes. The constant shuffling of feet caused him to involuntarily shiver. Even in the tropical heat, Pierre was feeling a chill.

The Africans were quietly heading below deck to an unrevealed place in the ship. It'd be for an unknown amount of time, by hostile captors, to sail to another unfamiliar destination for an unidentified purpose. Pierre couldn't imagine what all of that would be like.

Before, on the trip from France to Africa, when he and Captain Jean had talked about their future African cargo, they'd been nameless and faceless black commodities. Now it was different. There was fear, sadness, loss and quiet tears among the Africans he was watching. There was humiliation and abuse. He noticed scars and bloody wounds on the backs and chests of some of the people.

Then there was the smell. It was obvious these people had been in a place where they couldn't stay clean. Or, if they were uncivilized and pagan as the captain had claimed, maybe they didn't know how to clean themselves. He remembered how the captain had described the Africans as uneducated, poor and backward. Pierre had almost gotten to the point himself where he was expecting them to be like animals.

On the journey from Bordeaux to Africa, he was soaking up the training of his new sailor's education. The captain had taken a lot of time to share many things with him and he'd been thankful, almost proud of what he was learning. But now, the education was becoming entangled with his values. His mother had always taught him that people were equal. Obviously, some were more blessed than others, but all were equal in God's sight. Here, he was learning something different. He'd seen cows, pigs and sheep getting better care in France than these African men and women.

Especially difficult for him was watching boys and girls his age being treated as they were and exhibiting the scars of abuse.

Of all the emotions he was feeling, the most profound were guilt and shame. As the Africans climbed aboard the ship, he'd been standing along the gunwale eating a sandwich and holding a cup of water. Some of the African's eyes wandered to his food as they shuffled past. He'd quickly downed the remainder to ease his guilt.

As he followed a group of African men below-deck, the smell became stronger. Though they'd been washed before the sale, the odor of months of captivity weren't easily erased. It was then he wondered how these people would handle their personal needs. There had been no toilets or even buckets that he'd seen on the below decks. He'd seen hundreds of short chains secured to the gunwales, beams and floor boards. Their ominous use was clear.

As he descended to the second deck, he saw many men and women already secured. All were lying on the deck. There were bodies covering nearly the entire floor, stacked side by side like logs in a saw-mill yard. There were Africans crying and not all the cries were from the women.

He descended to the third deck which was half full. He watched as the ship's crew, along with a few African helpers, secured the men's neck collar to a chain fastened to the wall or floor. It appeared the chain was long enough for the men to sit, lay or stand if desired, but their space was still only six feet long by one and a half feet wide.

Again, the guilt and shame overwhelmed him. He knew tonight he'd have a soft mattress, blanket and pillow to sleep on. He couldn't imagine sleeping on a hard wooden deck for even one night. Then he thought of the three months they'd be on board until reaching Hispaniola. He decided to go up to the main deck to escape the guilt, shame and smells he was experiencing in the bowels of the ship.

On the main deck, the captain motioned for him to come to the helm. "Pierre, would you please bring me a cup of tea and a biscuit?"

Pierre headed to the galley, dodging the lines of African men still arriving. Now it was his turn to lower his head, not for fear of men, but wanting to shield his eyes from what he was seeing.

Arriving in the galley, he prepared the tea for the captain and collected two biscuits. Carrying it across the main deck, again, he had to pass through the line of Africans with the extravagances in his hands.

"Thanks Pierre. Did you get something to eat while you were there?"

"No, I'm not hungry."

"There will be time enough for that this evening. Tomorrow we set sail for Hispaniola. Are you ready?"

Pierre paused and found no words to respond.

The captain looked at Pierre with a knowing eye and said, "Ah Pierre. I think perhaps you're experiencing some things that unsettle you?"

Pierre kept his head lowered and said, "Yes, Captain."

"Well, you're reminding me of my first trip to the New World with a ship load of Africans. It was a difficult trip for me as I watched and learned. Over time, I've learned a lot. Once they arrive in Hispaniola, they'll like what they see. Hispaniola is much like Africa. Palm trees, sandy beaches, waterfalls, rivers and thick forests. Civilized people know we're rescuing the Africans from their poor, uneducated and uncivilized life and taking them to a new life which is much better. Others believe removing them from their worship of pagan gods and introducing them to the one true God is for their benefit. God knows that's true."

Looking at Pierre, the captain asked, "Does that help you to understand?"

"I suppose, but it's still difficult for me to watch what they're going through."

The captain looked at young Pierre and said, "Yes, I understand. Trust me, it'll get easier."

Pierre remembered the expressionless, unemotional and blank faces on the captain, surgeon and mates earlier and thought, *"I hope it doesn't get easier."*

~

As Pierre served the captain, surgeon and mates their evening meal, he listened to the conversation as the surgeon said, "I'm impressed with the condition of these Africans. This is as hardy a group as I've seen."

The captain responded, "I'd agree. As always, we'll need to be careful in taking good care of them. I talked to a Portuguese captain at the Castle who said he'd lost nearly one-third of his cargo on his most recent trip. Some type of fever had spread and he'd been concerned it'd claim everyone on board until they got it under control. Normally we'll lose fifteen per-cent on a voyage which is an acceptable number. More than that will definitely create a profit problem."

The first mate asked the captain, "I was wondering how many of these Africans we should use as cleaning crew for the crossing?"

"I think we'll use six of them. Rotate them with others so we don't wear any of them out prior to their sale. We'll use them for swabbing the manure from the lower decks. We need to stay ahead of that problem. Most of the African cargo will become sea-sick and their vomit and filth will be a seed bed for flies and disease."

"What about the African's exercise?"

"We can see how they fare, but they need to be brought to the main deck at least weekly for washing and exercise. We don't want to arrive in Hispaniola with weak, dirty, scrawny men and women. They need to be as healthy and clean as possible. After all, if they don't sell well, our profits will go down and we'll all suffer. As usual, make them dance so they get their exercise."

Pierre finished serving the dessert, but his mind was reeling. Absent-mindedly he served the sweet-cake to the men as he thought of the men and women below deck. It seemed the ship's crew considered the Africans the same as livestock or animals. He began thinking about what he was hearing from these men whom he'd started to respect. Was all of this for the African's spiritual benefit?

Was it for bringing them to a civilized condition? Was it about rescuing them from deep and dark Africa? Or, was it all about profit?

Pierre's mother had certainly taught him about right and wrong, good and evil, compassion and justice, but this experience was stretching all of those principles and values. Where was morality in all of this?

The men left and Pierre completed the clean-up of the dishes and silver. He was incredibly tired but knew it wasn't from the physical exertion of the day. He was emotionally exhausted as he crawled into bed.

In spite of the exhaustion, he was wide awoke. Tossing and turning, he thought of his mother. That brought emotions he hadn't felt for a few weeks. His mother had taught him to pray from the time he was a small boy and he automatically began whispering to God.

"Lord, I'm tired. I miss my mother and I know she misses me. Protect her until I return. I've seen so much on this trip and I don't know what to do with it. I pray that I won't get a hardened heart from seeing the things I've seen. Keep me soft. I'm more afraid of a hard heart than I am of the dangers on the open sea. Thank you for listening. In Jesus' name, Amen."

Sleep came quickly, as did dawn.

Chapter 26

May 20, 1777 – Cape Coast – The Gold Coast of Guinea

EKOW and Kwaku had a fitful night of sleep on the sandy beach. They both wondered how they'd explain the experiences of their nine days to their wives and the rest of the villagers.

They couldn't comprehend all that had happened nor all they'd experienced and felt. How could they possibly bring such horrible news to their Fante village? How could they explain to their wives that they'd seen Atu and Kisi in shackles and were unable to free them? How could they explain how other African men and women were helping in the capturing and selling of their own people?

They were feeling incredible shame and guilt. They couldn't describe the agony of seeing their children enslaved.

They'd watched their children board the *L'ange D'or* ship. Though they'd been on different wooden boats leaving shore at different times, they were at least together on the same ship. That gave Ekow and Kwaku a small degree of comfort.

Ekow said, "Kwaku, I'm thankful I didn't have to do this alone. I know my burden has been lighter since we're sharing this together."

"Yes, I know that's true. My father once told me, *'If you throw a spear at a zebra and it hits a dark stripe, the white stripe dies with it.'* We're together in this struggle. If you hurt, I hurt. I know our village people will walk alongside us when we tell them what's happened."

~

Kisi detested the heavy wrist shackle and the weighty chain attached to it, but what could she do about it? The sharp corners were cutting into her wrist. The rough deck board she was laying on pressed into her soft flesh. The whip-lash cut on her back was no longer bleeding but was still painful. No matter how she'd lay, she felt the heat of a body to her right and left. In some respects, feeling the bodies beside her, she knew she wasn't alone in this dark and smelly ship.

There was a bit of light filtering through portholes along the side. She looked up and saw three rectangular openings that permitted sunlight to enter. As she laid on the rough decking, she thought about how comfortable her hut had been. There, she had a mat to sleep on, food to eat, plenty of water, but most importantly, she had family.

Then, she thought of Atu. Those memories caused her to reflect back on their engagement and upcoming marriage. All of those plans died weeks ago when they were captured. She wondered where he was. The last time she saw him was in the courtyard during the sale. Was he still in the white building dungeon? Was he brought to one of the ships in the harbor? Was he on this ship or another one? Was he even alive?

Seeing her father at the shore had been a very bitter but sweet time and watching him get whipped was a memory she wouldn't forget. He could have remained quiet and simply watched, but he obviously wanted her to know he was there by calling out her name. She loved him for putting himself in danger and finding her. She saw love in his eyes as her boat inched its way across the bay to the ship.

She paused and listened to the sounds of the ship as she heard the heavy chains being reeled in from the ocean depths with their anchor in tow. Then the ship started to move. She desperately wanted to be on the main deck getting another glimpse of her father for the last time, but that wasn't going to happen.

~

Slowly Atu felt the ship begin to move. They'd been gently rocking in the calm harbor but now were definitely leaving Africa.

He cringed as he thought of his father being whipped across his face. Kwaku hadn't shown pain. He simply stood erect and watched as

Atu shuffled by. He was incredibly proud of his father and thankful for the unbelievable effort it'd taken for him to come to the oceans edge.

The ship was now moving faster and Atu listened to the noises aboard the ship. When it began moving, several men had cried out in desperation as they were facing yet more unknowns. Along with their cries, he heard the creaks and groans of the wooden planks making up this ship. He knew he'd hear those noises every day and every night for as long as he was onboard.

He wondered what had happened to Kisi. The last he saw her, she was leaving the white building. Was she on one of these ships? He'd seen her father Kwaku on the shoreline with his own father and was glad they could walk together through this tragedy.

When he'd been ushered below to the third deck, he got a glimpse of the floor completely covered with men and boys. Atu was pushed to the end of the deck where shelves were attached to the walls of the ship. He was roughly forced to the shelf. He climbed up and laid with his feet to the wall. Two feet above him was the ceiling. He knew he'd be unable to kneel, sit or stand. The guard attached a chain to his neck shackle. He felt desperately confined, helpless and hopeless.

Fear began to grow within him. From the deepest parts of his soul he began to feel frantic. If the ship sank in the ocean, there'd be no way to escape. He'd quickly drown.

How would he and the hundreds of others take care of their natural bodily functions? How would they be fed? What would they be fed? Would they be fed? The questions spilled out of his mind and fueled his fear.

Then, he thought to himself, *"I am Atu. I am a Fante warrior and tribesman. I've killed a bongo antelope with my own spear. I am a respected man of my village. A woman of great beauty has been chosen to be my wife. I've now survived some of the most horrible things put on a man. I will survive. I will live."*

The fear diminished as he thought of who he was. The fear was quickly replaced by a growing anger. It was an anger that had no recourse. He knew under normal circumstances anger would lead to action and retaliation. He knew he'd have to control his fear and anger or he'd go mad. He began his mantra again, *"I am Atu. I am a Fante warrior and tribesman. I've killed a bongo..."*

The anger subsided and was replaced again by helplessness and hopelessness. He knew his Fante mantra would need to be repeated in his mind a hundred times, a thousand times, or more.

~

Kwaku and Ekow continued watching the ship which their children had boarded and saw the white square cloths hoisted into place on the three branchless tree trunks. They listened to the clanking of iron chains as the bow anchors were raised. Then the ship began moving away from the shoreline.

They watched with a growing hopelessness as the ship became smaller and smaller on the horizon. Then it disappeared.

Both men had tear-filled eyes. There was nothing more they could do. There was nothing more to watch or wait for. They'd seen countless men, women and children taken into the white building and later taken to the ships.

Over the last nine days they'd talked to other Fante tribesmen in the seaside village. There'd been ideas about where the ships were sailing. Mostly they'd heard the Africans were being taken to faraway lands to work in the fields for the white men.

But there was another thing they'd heard more than once which was much more unsettling. They wished they'd not heard it, for it stuck in their minds. *'The white men are taking the Africans for food. They eat the dark meat.'*

With one last look at the oceans horizon, they began walking home.

Chapter 27

May 25, 1777 – Les Cayes, Saint-Domingue (now Haiti), Island of Hispaniola

FRANCOIS and his wife Marie sat on the Saint-Domingue beach watching their two boys playing in the sand. Dominic and Louis were eight and ten-years-old. A few feet away, Sylvain and Jeanne were watching their two girls playing in the nearby Caribbean surf. Inez and Louise were also ten and eight-years-old.

Their families were very close and spent a lot of time together, both during the week as well as on weekends. They lived on the same plantation but in two different houses. There weren't many white families in their area so their social circle was relatively small. In the entire country of Saint-Domingue, there were approximately 35,000 French people managing almost 500,000 African slaves.

There were several plantations in the Les Cayes area stretching from the Caribbean to the mountains in the north and the French families managing those various plantations were inter-connected. The elite and aristocratic families in France were a close-knit group and that extended to their mutual interests in Saint-Domingue.

A year ago, Francois and Sylvain made the very long and arduous trip by horseback to the capital city, Port au Prince, in central Saint-Domingue. Though the port city was only seven years old as the capital of the country, it was growing rapidly. The Caribbean port serviced the central portion of the country. They'd never seen so many ships in one location before.

As they strolled the docks, they saw hundreds of Africans. Some free-men, some slaves, all subservient to the few whites they saw. If a Frenchman fathered a child with an African woman, the child would be free. If a slave ran away, he could emerge elsewhere as a free man.

Many ships were bringing in thousands of Africans to serve the production needs of the many plantations. Most of the slaves would go to the huge valley plantations north of Port au Prince. The plantations in the south were served by the Les Cayes port.

While in Port au Prince, Francois and Sylvain found a French café frequented by the whites in the area. It was a refreshing stop after experiencing the busyness and smells of the busy docks and harbor.

Sitting at a table, they were soon joined by two other Frenchmen who were from a plantation north of Port au Prince. The four men had much in common as they traded stories and news from their areas.

One of the men asked, "So, how are the Africans doing in the south at Les Cayes? Are you hearing anything about rebellion?"

Sylvain replied, "No, they wouldn't dare revolt. We have the usual trouble-makers, but they're dealt with quickly. If we don't stop the individual problems, the trouble would multiply and soon be out of control."

"Well, in the north, we've had our problems. There are gangs of runaway slaves who've banded together in the mountains creating trouble. They're called Maroons. Unfortunately, there isn't anyone to control those wild animals. As long as they stay in the mountains, things remain peaceful, but periodically they raid the plantations. Sometimes they're able to free other slaves. They're a huge nuisance to us."

Francois looked at Sylvain and said, "I guess we can be thankful for how it's been going in the south. We'll need to watch for the trouble-makers or we'll have to learn how to deal with African gangs."

Sylvain nodded and then asked the two northerners, "So, what types of discipline have you found the most effective in keeping the trouble-makers under control?"

One of the men smiled and said, "Disciplining the trouble-makers with whippings helps, but the Africans are tough. They're getting used to the lashes. The best way to get their attention is by killing the rogue blacks when they show any sign of rebellion."

He continued, "When you kill the rebel, you have to do it in front of as many slaves as you can. The word will spread among them, you can be certain of that!"

Francois asked, "What have you found to be the best ways of getting their attention?"

The two northerners looked at each other. The older one replied, "Whatever you do, you need to do it without hesitation. Surprise them. Shock them. See what makes the onlookers vomit or cry. When you've done that, you know you've found the right methods."

Sylvain pushed them further, "I think we understand, but what do you do that gets their attention? We don't want to waste our time or the lives of our slaves with things that aren't effective. What are the things that work the best?"

"Well, since you're asking, we'll tell you what we've found has worked well. Gather a large group of slaves at the top of a hill. Push a rebel into a large rum barrel and nail on the cover. Let the other slaves watch you hammer thirty, long and heavy nails into the barrel through the sides. Take the group of slaves to the bottom of the hill. Then, roll the barrel to the bottom. Believe me, when you take the rebel out, you'll have the attention of all the slaves!"

The other man said, "Another thing we've found effective is putting a rogue in a sack and dropping him in the river. I also remember hearing from another plantation overseer about staking a rebel in the swamp to let the mosquitoes eat him alive."

Francois and Sylvain looked at each other. Francois said, "I think we understand."

One of the men from the north said, "If the plantation owners in the north had squashed the trouble when it started, we wouldn't have the problems we have. The only advice we have for you is to make sure you take care of the little problems before they become bigger. There are those nay-sayers who say that the French here in Saint-Domingue are the most vicious of all slave owners in history. But, that comes from people who have no idea what it's like to control the Africans."

When Sylvain and Francois arrived back home in Les Cayes, they began applying even stronger discipline on their slaves. They encouraged the nearby plantation managers to do the same. If just one of the plantations became soft, it'd soon become a problem for the rest.

The four children of Francois and Sylvain were now all having fun tumbling in the surf. Francois looked around. Directly ahead of him, across six miles of blue peaceful water he could see an island called *Ile-a-Vache* which meant *'Island of the Cows'*. Though he'd never been there, he knew the island had been a stronghold of British, Spanish and French pirates. There were sunken ships surrounding the island due to the shoals and reefs. As he looked toward the east there were miles of sandy beaches and palm trees. Twenty miles to the east were old Spanish and French forts. They'd been used to prevent pirates from stealing the bounty from the many ships using the port at Les Cayes.

To the west he could see a peninsula jutting out into the Caribbean. Everywhere there were palm trees along with mahogany, pine, catalpa, cypress and banana trees. The vegetation was lush and green. It was true, Saint-Domingue was truly a paradise!

In fact, the country had been named *'The Pearl of the Antilles'* by many due to its plentiful products of coffee, tobacco, indigo, sugar cane, pineapples and so much more. There was no doubt the abundance was profitable, but in reality, the wealth was borne on the backs of African slaves and the payments were made by African lives.

As the slow and relaxing day wore on, the two families began collecting their belongings. Their four black slaves resting under the palms took their cue and began hitching the horses to the two carriages for the trip back.

An hour later they entered the plantation gate and drove up the long lane, lined with palms and flowers, to their homes. The largest home belonged to the plantation owners, the Labreche family, who lived in Paris. The owners came to their plantation once a year for four weeks to be assured all was in order. Francois and Sylvain lived in smaller homes next to the large house.

The plantation's 1,000 African slaves lived in shanty huts a half mile behind the plantation homes. Those huts were made of dry palm leaves, sticks and mud.

As the Africans unloaded the carriage, Francois' family entered their comfortable and spacious home. Two full-time African maids kept it clean and provided plenty of fruit in bowls along with many pots of fresh-cut flowers. Francois smiled as he thought of the snow and ice that had plagued him seven years ago in France. Living in Saint-Domingue was truly a blessing. He sometimes couldn't believe his good fortune.

Along with a salary, he was provided with personal domestic servants, all his living expenses, plus an annual bonus from the plantation profits. His hot hours and days of toil in the fields of France seemed like a long time ago and far away. He smiled as he thought of the 1,000 plantation workers he had under his control and authority. He was becoming a wealthy and important man without the headache of owning land or property.

~

In the morning, Francois ate a leisurely breakfast with his family and emerged from his home to his waiting and saddled horse. He took the reins from his African slave and mounted. Waving to Marie, Dominic and Louis, he headed north toward the slave huts. He enjoyed these early morning rides. The sun hadn't yet begun its heated torment on the countryside and the day was fresh and smelled great. He loved how a night could reset the country from hot and sticky to something pleasant and new.

As he arrived at the secured slave village, he nodded to the two armed guards standing watch at the gate. Tall, impenetrable cactus surrounded the massive compound's 125 huts. There was no way a human or a dog could wriggle their way through the growth. The cactus had a poisonous milky substance which made it all the more menacing. If anyone got the substance in their eye, blindness was the ultimate result. The guards were responsible to keep the boundary fence impenetrable. If, upon inspection, there was an area larger than a six inch opening, there'd be a price to pay.

The guarded gate was the only way in and out. Walking the perimeter were eight more French guards as added security.

He periodically would personally inspect the compound fencing along with randomly inspecting huts to make certain no lingerers remained behind for non-valid reasons. He stopped in front of a shanty. Entering, he found it empty of the dozen inhabitants. There were no beds, only mats on the dirt floor. There were no chairs or tables so it was easy to see no one was left behind.

Holding the reins of his horse, he walked another twenty yards to another home and entered it. Empty.

Another ten yards and inspection. Again, empty.

He walked to a hut nearby where a woman and baby were sitting against the outside wall of the hut. She was nursing her newborn baby and kept her eyes lowered. Francois walked over to her and took the baby. Inspecting it closely, he noticed the infant was fat and healthy. If the child had been undernourished and weak, he'd have had Sylvain deal with it. There was simply no place on the plantation for needy children. Healthy ones would provide him with another worker in the future.

Entering the next hut, he saw a man lying on a mat in the corner. Stooping down, he realized the man was dead. He made a mental note to have one of the guards take care of the body. He smiled as he thought how these African slaves provided labor while living and fertilizer when dead. They were valuable commodities.

Finished with the inspection, he left the way he'd entered. Cantering the horse toward the east, he began walking his horse when he arrived at the sugar cane fields. He loved the smell of the cane when ripening and knew there would be many cartloads harvested today.

At the end of the cane field, he entered a massive clearing with several stone buildings. There were two hundred or so slaves working in this area along with eight white men who were overseeing them.

The cane carts were being unloaded beside a large stone wheel. The twenty ton wheel was massive at twelve feet in diameter and two feet thick. It stood upright in a stone trough. Water was being flushed through the trough along with the cane stalks which were crushed under the rotating huge wheel.

Francois remembered the man who had lost an arm two weeks earlier in this very spot. He looked around the yard for the evidence of that accident and saw a wooden post. Walking his horse toward the post he saw the arm still tied to it. The skin was as black as pitch and wrinkled from the hot sun. Insects had been busy and Francois saw white bone in spots. He was pleased to see this message would have an impact on the carefulness of his workers. Loss of a slave or downtime from an injury hurt the profits and ultimately his annual bonus.

Moving on, he walked his horse through the square mile of tobacco fields. Workers were cutting the tobacco while others were hanging it to dry in large barns. He galloped to the barns, dismounted and entered. He loved the smell of the drying tobacco. Moving slowly through the massive building he found what he was looking for. Reaching up he grabbed four of the now dry tobacco leaves. Putting them in his saddle bag for later, he was already savoring the opportunity to inhale their sweet smoke.

Then he heard a rustling. Quietly he moved toward a corner of the barn and saw a field-hand sleeping. He went to his horse and retrieved his whip. Approaching the slave, he lashed him again and again. The man, disoriented, stood, only to be pushed down and whipped again.

An overseer heard the screams of the slave and rode up to the barn. When he saw Francois and the black man, he dismounted. With his own whip, he continued the lashing.

Finally, the bloody African collapsed on the straw. Francois left the building and trusted the overseer to take care of business.

Though breathing hard from the exercise, Francois was, as always, exhilarated. Part of him enjoyed inflicting pain on the weak Africans.

Five minutes later he entered the cotton fields. The white fluff was evident throughout the fields as were the hundreds of workers picking the cotton. As he walked his horse through the rows, he noticed no one looking at him. He made a mental reminder to compliment Sylvain for training the slaves so well. If any of the slaves would have made eye contact, he'd have reported them as potential trouble-makers.

Men and women were busy filling their baskets. Once full, they carried them to a nearby cart, dumped the cotton and hurried back to continue their picking.

Francois got to the end of the fields and entered another meadow. A huge building had carts full of cotton bolls which were being dumped in front of a hundred women. The women were removing the seeds from the bolls. It was tedious, hot work but at least they were inside a building. Some of the women had a baby strapped on their back as they did their work. The children were tolerated as long as they remained healthy and didn't interfere with the woman working. If the child became a liability, it would be disposed of.

Along with the women were boys and girls who were as young as four-years-old. Their tiny fingers were efficient as they deftly picked seeds from the cotton. Francois smiled to himself as he thought how expensive it'd be to pay for all of this free slave labor. The Africans were truly a blessing for business enterprise!

On his way to the mahogany tree, he passed rice paddies in the plain which were in various stages of growth. Some of the paddies were ready for harvest, some had stubbles from a recent harvest and some were being prepared for planting. He saw several dozen men creating the mud paddies with their feet in preparation for planting the beginning stalks.

All the crops he'd just inspected needed water. Throughout the entire plantation the field hands had dug intersecting ditches. The water from the river, cisterns and artesian wells made its way to the various crops. There, men and women carried water to nurture them.

Francois was always amazed at what 1,000 men, women and children could accomplish if they had professional and experienced management. He made another mental note to have Sylvain provide additional rum to the French workers who provided the expertise to make all of this successful.

Arriving at the mahogany tree, he dismounted and tied his horse to a long rope, giving him plenty of grazing area.

Opening his saddlebag, he retrieved his bottle of rum, the tobacco leaves, some fruit and a venison sandwich. Settling in for a few hours of management work, he began eating his sandwich.

Washing down the venison with rum, he pulled his well-used clay pipe from his vest pocket. Breaking up a tobacco leaf which had been drying for six weeks, he tamped it into the pipe and lit it. Inhaling the sweet smoke, he leaned his head back against the tree.

Right on time, Sylvain arrived and settled in beside him. Francois made the rum and tobacco available and they spent an hour talking business.

"Ah, another day in paradise."

Francois responded, "Yes it is, my friend. With God's help and blessings it should go on forever!"

Sylvain smiled.

Chapter 28

May 27, 1777 – On Board the *L'ange D'or* Slave Ship

ON the first day at sea, since leaving Cape Coast, Atu vomited. The never-ending pitching and rolling of the ship created a new horror. Up, down, to one side, then the other, was almost more than he could bear.

He felt incredibly sick. He'd tried to stop retching, but it was impossible. If only he could have stood and walked around, he thought he could have warded off the cramps, nausea and vomiting. The first time it happened he was self-conscious. After two minutes, he no longer thought about anyone else or anything else. His vomiting was the only thing on his mind. His stomach ached terribly.

He wasn't alone in his misery. The sounds of vomiting were coming from all directions. Sounds of misery. They were the audible sounds of fear and terror. He knew the bitter and vile contents of his stomach, though meager, were splattering on those closest to him, just as theirs were splashing on him.

After thirty minutes his stomach began to slowly, almost imperceptibly, settle. The smell of vomit was in the air, along with the strong stench of urine and excrement. His own bowels had released along with his bladder and he felt the coarse boards under him becoming wet and slippery. The horrors of the white castle dungeons were now being relived as the same smells began permeating the air.

Though it'd now been one week on the water, it seemed time had almost stopped. Was there no end to this agony? The vomiting and nausea was never far away. Though he was learning to control it to some degree, he wasn't always successful. The smells in the hold were only getting stronger and worse. That, of course didn't help his nausea. The amount of feces, urine and vomit was growing as it turned into a vile slurry on the deck below him.

At first, he'd been angry to have been laying on the shelf with very little room above him. Now he was thankful. If he were on the flat deck floor, the slurry would be under and around him.

The floor boards above him were dripping the same thick liquid from the deck above where the women and other men were located. At least in the dungeon he'd kept his head dry and relatively clean. After the dungeon experience in the Castle, he'd thought nothing could get worse. But this was a new low. Lying on his back created the hazard of drips onto his face or into his mouth. Lying on his stomach put his face next to the liquid on the shelf deck he was laying on.

He could keep track of the days and nights. The nights were pitch black. During the day, slivers of light entered the hold by which he could make out the forms of the other tormented souls close to him.

From the sounds being made throughout the days and nights, he discerned there were many, many men on this deck with him. Periodically he'd hear a Fante word or phrase.

He couldn't count the number of times he'd uttered his mantra...

"I am Atu. I am a Fante warrior and tribesman. I've killed a bongo antelope with my own spear. I am a respected man of my village. A woman of great beauty has been chosen to be my wife. I've now survived some of the most horrible things put on a man. I will survive. I will live."

His desire to survive was paramount. Nothing else mattered. If he failed to survive, all that he'd experienced would become useless. There had to be good things that would come from all of this hell.

Inevitably, his thoughts would gravitate to thinking about Kisi. *Was she alive? Was she still in the white Castle? Did she make it to one of the ships? If so, which ship?*

Then, he'd think of his family and village. *How did they react to the news Ekow and Kwaku had brought them? How was his mother doing? Had the villagers already forgotten his success as a hunter?*

Had he gone in their minds from a mighty hunter to simply a man who couldn't protect his betrothed?

The nausea returned. He turned off his thinking and retched.

~

Kisi couldn't resist crying. Throughout their week at sea, she'd already experienced so much. The violent vomiting came and went and the nausea had never totally left. The lurching of the ship was creating sore spots all over her body and caused the iron shackle on her wrist to chafe. Though she couldn't see it, she thought her wrist might be bleeding. She wasn't sure if the dampness on her wrist was blood or urine. It was stinging, so likely it was urine in an open wound.

There was so much crying around her. She could constantly hear men and women pouring out their tear-filled misery. She knew she was surrounded by many people. She'd hoped that somehow, someway she'd be close enough to Darifa to have someone to touch and whisper to, but it didn't happen. Yet, in the hold, she could have been ten feet away and neither would have known. She missed their closeness.

Someone had opened the top deck hatches to let ocean air and light filter into the hold. Periodically, buckets of ocean water were thrown through the hatch openings. It only seemed to add to the slop which was constantly splashing around her.

Daily, crew members entered the hold and brought food. It was a pasty gravy of sorts that she had to eat with her dirty fingers. The bread they brought was hard and crusty but it was food. Buckets of fresh water were carried in and handfuls were divided out to each person.

One day after receiving their food and water, something new happened. The crew began unshackling the chains of the women at the other end of the ship. They climbed the stairway to the main deck.

African men then entered the hold with buckets of water and began scrubbing the deck where the women had been. They pushed the slurry through the scupper holes at the deck floor which drained to the sea. Thirty minutes later, the women returned to a relatively clean deck, were re-shackled and another thirty or so women went up the stairway.

Finally, Kisi's turn came. Again she felt fear of the unknown, but getting out of this hole for thirty minutes seemed like a good thing. A crewman unlocked the chain from her wrist iron. Kisi stood and immediately fell heavily to the floor. She didn't know if it was her weak legs or the slippery deck. Regaining her footing, she followed the other women to the main deck.

As she emerged into the bright sunshine, she stopped. Looking around, she saw only water. Their ship was on the ocean. She'd never seen anything like it! Suddenly she was pushed forward by a crewman. She wondered what was coming next.

Buckets of sea water were being used to wash the women. Each of them stood naked as they washed the grime of their first week at sea from their bodies.

Kisi looked at her wrist. It was oozing blood. She knew she needed to get it clean and she'd need to be more careful how she handled her shackle.

It was now her turn. Despite the ogling and laughing of the ships crewmen, she tilted her head back and soaked up the sunshine and began removing the filth. She couldn't believe how she'd taken water for granted before becoming captive. In the area where she'd lived, water was always available. Now it was as precious as gold.

Suddenly there was a commotion. One of the women broke away from the group. Running to the side of the ship, she tried to jump over the side. However, there were nets made from rope stretched along the sides above the gunwale that prevented her from succeeding. The woman screamed in frustration and terror as she was grabbed by two crewmen who held her tightly. A third came with a short whip which he whipped her with, again and again. The screaming stopped when her body went limp. She fainted. The whipping continued.

Kisi knew the desperation the woman must have felt. The woman would have chosen drowning and death instead of returning to the hell-hole in the bottom of the ship.

A crew member doused the prostrate woman with a bucket of ocean water. With a gasp the woman revived. Kisi heard a low moan coming from the woman's parted lips. It seemed to be coming from somewhere deep inside. The moan continued until a crewman kicked her in the side.

Everyone watching quickly learned the rules of being aboard the *L'ange D'or*. No eye contact. No talking. If disobedience happened, discipline would be quick, long and harsh.

Filing back to the stairway, they descended to their chains and were shackled. Kisi was grateful for the newly washed slot which had become her home. Carefully she adjusted the location of her wrist shackle to prevent further damage to her wound.

She paused and listened. The deck had grown silent. The women seemed to be more accepting of their situation. She was amazed how contented people could be when having so little.

Then, the exodus of men to the top deck began. Half of the Africans on her deck were men and she watched in the filtered light as they filed up the stairs.

She strained to see if any of the men were Atu. *Was he alive? Was he still in the white building or was he on a ship? Was he on this ship?*

Not recognizing anyone, she hung her head and quietly cried.

~

Pierre watched as the African women and now men arrived on the main deck of the *L'ange D'or*. The stench of the holds had arrived on deck with the African slaves. Gradually, the ocean breeze and the

Atlantic seawater permeated the odor. He watched as the clean water pouring out of the buckets hit their heads, washed their bodies and pooled on the main deck in brown puddles. He'd nearly vomited because of the smell emanating from the Africans.

He watched as the men used the buckets of water to wash themselves. He saw them raise their heads to the sun for a moment. He noticed some looking at the ocean seeking a glimpse of their Africa, to no avail.

The men weren't chained. There were so many guards with whips, swords and pistols standing around, Pierre knew an African mutiny wouldn't be happening.

He was startled as he watched an African shove one of the guards and run to the side of the ship. The man headed to a spot in the rope netting which had a larger than normal hole. He plunged through the hole and disappeared over the side. Pierre ran to the starboard side and saw the man bobbing in the blue waves of the Atlantic. The winds quickly pushed the ship past the man as he disappeared from sight. His troubles were over.

The captain hollered to the first mate to join him at the helm. He uttered a quick command and the first mate walked among the crew until he found who he was looking for. Grabbing a crewman by his shirt, the first mate pulled him to the mizzenmast. Pulling off the man's shirt he raised his whip and brought it down hard on his back. Again and again and again. His back was bleeding from the lacerations. He fell to the deck moaning and bleeding.

The first mate told the crew, "This man was responsible for the rope net. He failed and the loss of a slave is without excuse." He pointed to another crew member and said, "From now on, the rope nets are your responsibility. If we lose another slave, you'll go over the side... after you've taken your whipping."

The slaves gaped at the bloody white man on the deck. Pierre could see fear go through the group. He knew what they were thinking. *'If the boss leader could do this to a white man, what would he do to a black man?'*

Pierre looked at Captain Jean. He saw someone different than the captain he thought he knew.

The washing of the African men continued all afternoon. Finally, the job was completed and the deck was now nearly empty. Pierre sat on the stair steps at the helm and looked toward the bow of the ship. There were eight large copper kettles cooking food for the slaves.

His gaze shifted to the gunwales where he counted twelve large cannon. Next to them were racks of three inch diameter cannon balls. Though he'd have loved to watch them fire, he hoped there would never be a need. Subconsciously he scanned the horizon for a ship. He knew the cargo below decks would be a high value treasure for pirates.

A few days earlier, Pierre had a conversation with the captain who said, "Pirates patrol these waters and they sometimes prefer taking a slave ship rather than a ship with other goods. Slaves are a treasure. Believe me, in the Caribbean, the pirates have no problem in selling a fresh slave."

He looked over the bow at the bowsprit pointing toward Saint-Domingue on Hispaniola. They only had one week of twelve behind them.

He headed to the galley to prepare the table for the captain, his mates and the surgeon. As usual, Pierre learned a lot about life and particularly sea-life by listening to the dinner conversations.

Clement the surgeon said, "Captain, I'm concerned by what I saw when the men and women were on the main deck. We've been out only seven days and I'm seeing some mighty thin and weak slaves. What did you think?"

"I'd agree, but I'm not overly concerned. They take a while to acclimate to ship-life. I think their sea-sickness is about over. They'll get their sea-legs under them quick enough."

Dr. Clement continued, "We'll need to watch for dysentery. Even in the best of conditions, by the time we get to Saint-Domingue we'll likely lose about seventy-five of our 450."

The captain responded, "Aye, likely so. Starting this week, let's daily bring up sixty or seventy for washing and check their health. That'll give each group an opportunity to come above weekly. That should be easier for the crew, rather than doing it all in one day."

The first mate said, "If I could be so bold, Captain Jean, I have another question?"

"Aye?"

"When will you be assigning us our token black?"

"I'll do that as we near the end of the voyage."

Looking at the third mate who was new to the ship, Captain Jean said, "I know every ship's captain is different. But on the *L'ange D'or*, the first mate knows that each of you and the surgeon will be getting a bonus for the trip. Each of you will receive one of the slaves as your own. You can sell him or work him, the choice is yours. I'll wait until the end of the journey. It'd be a sad thing if the one you picked now would decide to jump over the rail or maybe died of dysentery."

Pierre served a sugared dessert to the men and retrieved a bottle of rum from the captain's supply. They continued their banter and Pierre began the clean-up process. Soon they headed to their berths with the exception of the second mate who took the helm.

Pierre was exhausted as he sank into his bed. His tallow candle cast an eerie light on the swaying walls of the hallway leading to the captain's quarters. He blew it out but was surprised to still see flickering shadows on the wall. Looking down the short hall, he saw the first mate coming toward him with a candle. The mate filed past with someone behind him.

A young black woman with a rope around her neck was being led past him toward the captain's quarters. There was a sharp rap-rap on the door which opened quickly. The captain stepped aside and the mate and African woman entered. Almost immediately the mate left.

Pierre shut his eyes and again uttered his mantra...

"Lord, I'm tired. I miss my mother and I know she misses me. Protect her until I return. I've seen so much on this trip and I don't know what to do with it. I pray that I won't get a hardened heart from seeing the things I've seen. Keep me soft. I'm more afraid of a hard heart than I am of the dangers on the open sea. Thank you for listening. In Jesus' name, Amen."

~

The next morning, Pierre finished his chores and climbed the stairway to the main deck.

Listening to the sounds of the ship, he heard the wind filling the sails. The sails sometimes made a snapping sound as the wind hurtled into them and thrust them forward toward Hispaniola. The captain had told him that God was blessing the Atlantic slave trade by providing trade winds pushing them from Africa to the Caribbean. When Pierre stood at the helm and looked westward, his back usually felt the wind. They were moving quickly through the dark Atlantic waters. The captain had said, "It's God's will for the educated English and Europeans to do what we do for the Africans. He's provided the trade winds as a sign of His good will and blessing."

He smelled the pleasant odor of food emanating from the large cooking pots on the bow. The ocean-fresh air was something he enjoyed, but even on deck he could smell the stink of the Africans drifting upward from the holds below.

Looking starboard he saw at least ten dolphins tracking the ship. Keeping up with the ship seemed impossible, but they were. Jumping often out of the water, it seemed they were putting on a performance just for him. He smiled.

The captain relieved the first mate at the helm and hollered to Pierre, "Come join me, my lad."

Pierre spent as much time as possible with the captain. He was the nearest person to a father he might ever have again. But today, Pierre was reluctant to go to the helm. With another glimpse at the dolphins, he slowly walked to the captain who noticed his reluctance.

The captain watched him as Pierre stood beside him. "Want to take the wheel?"

Pierre grabbed the spokes and held them tightly in his hands while staring intently ahead.

"Pierre, did you sleep well?"

"Yes, sir. I did."

"Good. I want to talk to you about something."

Pierre continued staring over the bowsprit.

"Have I ever told you about my family?"

"No sir, you haven't."

"I have a wife in Paris and we have three sons. Over the next five years, they'll graduate from secondary school. They hope to go on to a university. I'm sad to say that none seem to have an interest in the sea. I suppose my absence from them during their growing-up years hasn't set well with them."

Pierre listened as the captain continued.

"My time at sea has provided very well for my family. They've had everything that money could buy."

Pierre wondered why the captain was sharing all of this with him.

"You may have wondered why a black girl came to my cabin last night?"

Pierre said nothing.

"Were you awoke when she arrived?"

Waiting a few seconds, Pierre finally said, "Yes sir, I was."

"I'd like to explain something to you. Being away from home for so many months can make a man lonely. I'm simply human. I had the first mate find a young woman to take away some of my loneliness. Do you understand? It's difficult being away from my wife for so long."

Pierre hesitated, then said, "When I'm lonely, I find someone like you or one of the other cabin boys to talk to. I don't see how this girl could help your loneliness since you and she can't speak the same language."

"Ah, my boy. You're not only an inquisitive young man, you're also wise beyond your years. Yes, there's more to satisfying loneliness than talking. Companionship goes in many directions."

Pausing, he continued, "This African girl has been through so much. Her time with me was a reprieve for her from the darkness of the hold. I gave her some food to eat while she was with me. Though she couldn't tell me, I believe I helped her and she was thankful."

Pierre was glad he was busy steering the ship as it seemed to give him an excuse to look away from the captain and remain quiet.

"The officers on board also do their part in helping some of the girls have a little something extra. You'll see that happening fairly often on our trip west."

The captain paused, looked at Pierre and continued, "I just wanted to explain the situation to you."

Bordeaux, France where Pierre grew up was a seafaring city. He hadn't grown up ignorantly and didn't need the captain's explanation.

The captain took over the wheel and Pierre headed for the stairway to the second deck as African men were arriving for their weekly washing and sunshine.

Stopping halfway down the staircase, he sat and peered into the flickering darkness. The hold hatches above were open so slivers of light filtered through. There were openings on the sides where the side canvas caught a breeze and brought in cool air to the slaves.

Only six feet away from him to his left was a man. He saw a black face and white eyes peering back for just a moment. Then the eyes turned away. The smell was horrible in the hold, but his curiosity overcame his need to find fresh air.

Looking to his right, he saw a young girl watching him. He smiled at her and she looked away with fright in her eyes. He watched her and was sad his presence created fear.

Then, a loud commotion from above broke his concentration on the situation of the Africans before him. As he emerged from the stairway, he heard men shouting, followed by a musket-shot.

There were about sixty African men on deck. At the bow, the captain and two crewmen were looking down at a man. Pierre walked toward the group.

Lying in a pool of blood, an African lay dead. His head was mangled from the gunshot. Pierre looked at the face of the captain. It was blood splattered and full of anger. In his right hand was a smoking flintlock pistol. Pierre could smell the black-powder smoke in the air, mingled with the salty sea-air and the iron smell of blood.

The captain started to walk to the helm and through clenched teeth muttered to the crewmen, "Clean this mess up!"

A crewman unlashed the security netting. Two of the men grabbed the arms and legs of the African and carried him to the gunwale. Swinging him in perfect rhythm as if they'd done this often, they tossed the man into the Atlantic.

Buckets of sea-water were quickly thrown on the bloody mess and the deck was scrubbed. The life of another African was swept from the deck of the *L'ange D'or*, through the side-scuttle, into the Atlantic and gone forever.

Pierre looked around and saw another cabin boy. "What happened?"

"Oh, the African men were on deck and one of them looked at the captain who was nearby. The captain slapped him. The man got closer and stared into the captain's eyes. The captain slapped him again. The African was acting crazy-like or maybe he just wanted to die. The third time the African glared at the captain, he pulled his pistol and shot him in the head."

The boy laughed, "You won't see any of the other African heathens looking at the captain like that!"

Chapter 29

June 3, 1777 – On Board the *L'ange D'or* Slave Ship

CAPTAIN Jean was in his quarters at noon. There never seemed to be enough time to get all of his tasks completed.

The owners of the *L'ange D'or* in Paris had been incredibly kind to him over the years as he faithfully fulfilled his contracts. The tasks were simple for the most part. Load the ship with goods and cargo in Bordeaux; sail to the Gold Coast of Guinea, Africa; unload the cargo; purchase slaves and transport the cargo to Hispaniola; load the ship with Hispaniola products and sail back to Bordeaux, France.

The process was fairly methodical and he'd done it many times. The difficult issues were the unforeseen things such as a potential mutiny of his crew or the Africans themselves, yellow fever, dysentery, storms or piracy. Those things kept him on his toes.

Then, of course, he needed to keep records of slaves purchased and of deaths aboard ship. He had to minimize the loss of slaves and crew as well as the amount of cargo consumed enroute. He needed to maintain the crew records, all of the navigational plotting records and try to maintain some degree of order among a rough and motley crew.

Early that morning he'd noticed a swelling of clouds to the northeast. Typically the strongest trade winds came from the northeast over Africa and pushed westward. Another set of trade winds blew out of the southeast over southern Africa and also pushed westward. When a storm developed, those winds were merciless in pushing storms quickly over the Atlantic water. He'd watched this morning as the storm clouds continued to grow higher and expand behind them extending to the north and south. He knew within a day, they'd be experiencing this voyage's first storm.

After two weeks on the open ocean, the crew and slaves had settled into a routine that seemed to be going well. However, a storm would test the courage of the crew and the durability of the African stock housed below.

The captain hollered, "Pierre, come here."

Pierre had been doing chores outside the captain's quarters and entered almost immediately. "Yes sir. What do you need?"

"Pierre, we'll most certainly be experiencing a storm this evening or sometime during the night. We need to be ready. This'll be your first storm. Are you ready for it?"

"I'm not sure, sir. What should I do?"

"It'll probably happen after our supper so make sure all the dishes, utensils and cookware are cleaned and stored in the secure cabinets. The furniture is already bolted to the floor so we won't worry about that. The biggest thing will be to ready yourself for a frightening night. We'll be alright, but during the storm you'll think the devil himself is aboard this ship."

Pierre left the captain and had a chill go through his body as he wondered what might be ahead.

~

Kisi felt squashed in her little area nestled between four other women. One to her right, another to the left and still others by her head and feet. The continual rocking of the ship no longer made her nauseous. She was thankful she could stand, sit or kneel periodically to stretch her legs and arms.

Though humiliating and only happening weekly, the washing on the main deck was wonderful. It felt like a breath of freedom when she entered into the sunlit skies above deck. She always returned to her space feeling fresh and renewed.

Now, as she lay on the rough, splintered, wet and slippery planking she again wondered where Atu might be. Dead? Alive in the Castle or on a ship? Which ship? Would she ever see him again?

As she'd watched the wooden boats taking slaves to the various ships in the harbor, she thought of the impossibility of seeing him again. There were simply too many slaves on too many ships, likely going to different places.

The slaves had received their meal at noon and she knew nothing more would come until the next day. She rested her head on the planking beneath her and relaxed. As she rocked from side to side, she began remembering another time...

Her mother's sister had her second baby. A beautiful little girl they'd named Efia. Often, Kisi's responsibility as a young girl had been to care for her cousin when the mothers went to their gardens.

One warm afternoon, Efia began crying and Kisi had no success in getting her to stop. Nothing she'd tried would work so she climbed into a hammock strung between two palm trees with the baby on her lap. The hammock began swinging and soon little Efia became quiet and fell asleep. It wasn't long before Kisi had fallen asleep as well.

It was a sweet memory as she lay on board the ship in the middle of a vast ocean. Soon, the rocking motion of the ship put her to sleep.

~

Atu awoke to someone screaming. It took him a moment to realize he wasn't dreaming as he felt gripped by darkness and penetrating fear. Periodic explosions of thunder and flashing lightning illuminated the black faces of those near him. He was struck by the intense terror he saw in their eyes and knew he was no different.

The ship was tossing from side to side. The screaming of near and distant men, women and children was increasing. The ship's wooden planking was groaning and straining. It seemed as if the ship itself was in a death throe and gripped by something much larger than itself. It reminded him of the bongo antelope he'd speared so many months ago. He'd watched it slowly and surely die, but only after thrashing amidst the ferns and greenery of the jungle floor. Death was inevitable and final.

The old familiar nausea returned to his stomach and soon he joined others in vomiting their last meal. The thunder, lightning flashes, screaming, vomiting, the ever-present sliding on the deck boards, all contributed to the fear welling within him. Then the ship plunged deep into a wave trough and he felt as if he were falling. Suddenly the ship hit the bottom of the trench and began its rise upward. It was then his head hit the bulwark, hard, and he slipped into unconsciousness.

~

Pierre saw fear in the eyes of some of the sailors in the galley and his personal shame began to dissipate as he knew he wasn't alone in his terror. He sat on the floor and held the secured table leg tightly as the ship tossed and rolled in the wild Atlantic. He wondered how the African cargo was faring, but only for an instant as once again the ship rose higher and higher, only to plunge to the other side of yet another mountainous wave.

He'd given up several hours earlier, in trying to keep his supper down. Yielding to the nausea, he'd been ashamed of his weakness in front of the sea-worn sailors. But, they hadn't laughed, for which he was thankful.

He noticed one of the cabin-boys silently crying. Again, there was no laughter from the crew. It was then Pierre knew this was indeed a bad storm. It'd been going on for hours.

Holding the table leg in a death grip, he looked toward the stairway leading up to the main deck. Water was spilling down the steps and disappearing to the sea through some unseen gunwale scuttle ports. He wondered if it were his imagination, but it seemed the storm was beginning to moderate.

Two of the crewmen slowly made their way to the steps and disappeared into the darkness above. He followed carefully. Emerging onto the deck he was mesmerized by the lightning flashes, the sounds of thunder and incredible pounding rain. He got a glimpse of Captain Jean and the first mate in their oil-skin slickers at the helm before he retreated below. He'd seen enough.

After another twenty minutes, the storm had pushed itself ahead into the west and calm gradually returned to the ocean and the ship. It was now well past midnight, but sleep was far from his mind.

He went to the helm and saw a haggard and exhausted captain. Captain Jean smiled at Pierre through the lantern-lit darkness. "Well boy, how did you fare?"

"I've never been so scared in my entire life!"

"Ah, I understand. The demons of hell are unleashed on such a night as this, are they not?"

He continued, "Well, Pierre, you may as well get some sleep. The morning will soon enough shine its light on work waiting to be done."

~

At first light, Pierre left his damp bed to get a glimpse of a new day. The sun was just rising in the east amidst a beautiful orange sky. He looked around and saw men already repairing torn and ripped sails. The side canvases designed to bring air to the lower decks of Africans were tattered. Crewmen were sent to dismantle those which were torn to bring them to the main deck for repair.

Pierre nearly laughed out loud when he saw rough, scarred and tough seamen, sitting on the deck, with awls in their hands sewing the material. Maybe they weren't so different from the housewives in Bordeaux. Then he smiled as he knew they were nothing like the ladies back home. He quickly dropped the smile for fear one of the men would think he was making fun of him. Then he thought of his mother and knew last night's experience was yet another piece of his education he needed to report to her.

He paused and smelled the air. Fresh. He descended the stair steps to the next deck to see how the Africans had fared in their first storm.

He was struck by the quietness. The morning sun was penetrating the darkness enough to see the masses of men, women and children. The ever-present smell penetrated his nostrils and again became a part of his memory. He knew he'd never forget the smells aboard this ship.

As he sat on the step, lingering, his eyes met the eyes of one of the African men. Normally, they'd quickly divert their eyes, but this time, the African eyes were exploring him.

Pierre wondered what they saw. He assumed they considered him safe due to his youthfulness. He'd never threatened or harmed them. He was sure they'd noticed.

He thought back to two months earlier when he'd first boarded the ship and how his mother had watched with sad eyes as her only child walked the gangplank to the L'ange D'or.

What had she felt as her son was taken from her, through no fault of his own? He knew she'd been extremely sad. He knew beyond a doubt she was afraid for him, yet praying for his safety and return.

As he looked deeper into the African's black eyes he saw emotion. Fear. Anger. Frustration. Emotions.

What were their families thinking in Africa when these men, women and children were kidnapped? Did the mothers and fathers of these Africans experience sadness as his own mother had? Were the pagan and backward African people capable of thinking and feeling just as the Europeans did?

Suddenly it struck him! He was thinking of the Africans as human beings. He knew there were mothers, fathers, sisters and brothers mourning the loss of those they loved.

Pierre's eyes filled with understanding and compassion. Then he felt the tears come. Wiping them, he turned around and headed to the upper deck.

Chapter 30

June 20, 1777 – On Board the *L'ange D'or* Slave Ship

PIERRE was busy cleaning the captain's quarters. Pausing in front of a small mirror, he peered at his image. He couldn't believe how much he'd changed since he left his mother in Bordeaux on April 11th, over two months earlier.

His hair was long, over his ears and down his neck. His face was bronzed, scarred and the freckles he'd sported in France had now disappeared. His blue eyes weren't quite as innocent as they'd been before. He wondered if his mother would recognize him when he returned in another few months.

The time aboard the ship had a rhythm and routine that became almost monotonous. They'd now been on the high seas of the Atlantic for four weeks since leaving Guinea. He knew in another eight weeks they'd arrive on Hispaniola and he wondered what else would happen to break up the monotony.

The storm had certainly changed things for him. He'd never felt so much fear. The captain had said they'd likely experience another two or three storms before arriving at port and most would be worse than the first. Pierre wasn't looking forward to that.

He thought of other abnormal things that had happened thus far. There had been four Africans who had jumped overboard. He thought of others who had tried jumping without success and were beaten. He remembered the crewmen who were beaten for carelessness in letting the jumpers succeed.

The captain had said, "Pray for boredom, but be prepared for the worst."

He was thankful his mother had raised him with a love for God and a dependence on Him. He knew the values and principles she'd taught him were helping him cope with what he was seeing, hearing, smelling and experiencing. The prayer he was reciting everyday helped to reinforce his beliefs.

Even so, he was surprised that he seemed to be the only one on board the ship with morals, principles and values. Listening to the rough language of the crewmen was simply a part of life aboard ship. Though he heard the names of God and Jesus mentioned often in conversations, he knew the names were uttered as curses. He wondered how many voyages were needed to erase God from the minds of men. Already he'd witnessed more about life, death and evil than most men see in a lifetime.

That evening as he crawled into his berth, he silently prayed his prayer. Then he added, *"...and Lord, I don't want to become like these other men on board the ship. They've lost You and maybe never knew You. I pray that You'll keep me close."*

~

The next day began as Pierre woke at dawn and groggily went to the main deck. He was surprised to see the dark skies and feel a gusty wind. Looking at the helm, he saw the first mate grasping the wheel, so he quickly joined him and stood facing the bow. The wind was blowing hard at his back.

"Pierre, it looks like we're in for another nor'easter. That should keep life exciting for the next day or two."

Pierre felt a deep chill slide across his back. He knew it wasn't just the wind from Africa blowing on him. He felt the storm-fear gripping him. Looking over the gunwale, he saw the swells getting larger.

The crew was beginning to prepare the ship for a long day and night on a rough sea. Some were dismantling the sails. Others were checking and battening down barrels, cannons and cannon balls. Anything loose on the decks could become a missile plunging through the gunwale and threatening the ships ability to stay afloat.

He knew there were men on the decks below readying the cargo. The Africans wouldn't fly about, as they were chained in place.

Pierre went below and prepared breakfast for the captain and mates and made sure the table and chairs were battened to the deck. The first storm had taught him a lot. There was nothing like being in a storm aboard ship to educate seamen quickly as to what needed to be done, so he completed his chores hastily.

The captain and mates hurried in for a quick breakfast. Tension was in the air as they spoke of what was to come. Captain Jean said, "I'm afraid this one has the makings of a devil. It's come up quickly and I doubt it'll be over anytime soon."

After washing the dishes and utensils, Pierre did a second check to make sure everything was secured. Then he went topside to view a much darker sky and heavier wind. There was no rain as yet, but the air had the smell of freshwater.

He turned to look over the stern of the *L'ange D'or* in the direction of Africa. He remembered the captain saying the trade winds were from God and blessed their slaving work. Pierre asked himself, '*I wonder what the captain is thinking now with this wind and upcoming storm? Greater blessings? I don't think so!*'

The first drops of rain splattered on his face. He decided to go below. He didn't need to see the fury of another storm. He just hoped they'd survive it. He was incredibly thankful for the captain's confidence and experience on the ocean.

~

The storm unleashed its fury that dark afternoon. There was no indication the sun was above them as black clouds and torrential rain obscured it from view. Once again, Pierre saw the veiled fear on the faces of the crew and the not-so-veiled fear on the faces of the cabin boys. Would anyone ever get accustomed to these Atlantic storms?

The storm continued into the evening. There wasn't any reprieve from the continual tossing and turning. Pierre couldn't imagine how the captain and mates could stay on their feet at the open-air helm in this driving rain and wind. The art of keeping the ship parallel with the storm could only come with years of hard earned experience.

The howling wind and persistent rolling of the ship was a terror in itself. The panic which came from the endless drops into the deep furrows between each wave was enough to bring him to the edge of horror each time. Then, almost immediately the ship would begin its upward journey to, yet again, the top of another monstrous wave.

And so it went, for hours on end. Pierre wondered how the Africans were faring, but soon forgot them as the ship plunged downward again.

Suddenly, something changed. The motion of the ship was different. He knew the helmsman was struggling to keep the ship lined up with the storm. The ship lurched deeply to the starboard side and he knew they were heading sideways into a trench. He felt the ship plunging and then it hit the bottom of the valley.

For what seemed too long, the captain was finally able to prevent the *L'ange D'or* from capsizing. It was then Pierre knew how to pray in desperation. What is it when the terrors of the unknown strike, that drives man ultimately to bargaining with God?

His quick and sincere prayer had been simple. *"Please get us safely through this storm. I'll serve you wherever and however you want for the rest of my life!"*

~

Kisi's wrist was raw. Each time the ship plummeted into the next valley, her body slid forward, stopped only by the chain on her wrist. Then there was a sudden jerk on the chain when the ship hit the bottom. Then, again and again. The pain in her hand, arm and wrist was excruciating, never-ending.

The hold was as black as she'd ever seen it. Always, there was the constant wetness from above as water struggled to find its way down into the ship and then to the scuttle ports. On the bright side, she was thankful for each new surge of water which would carry the feces and vomit to the ocean. Would this ever end? The screams of horror, the crying of children and even adults, and the continual vomiting were all contributing to this hell-hole.

Her anger and hatred for the white men was growing daily. During the storm it was growing with each wave of nausea she felt and with each new wave they climbed. *How could any human being treat another man like they were being treated? Beyond that, how could any man treat women and children as they were being treated?*

She'd never imagined the world was so large or that it had such wickedness in it. Her Fante world had been perfect and predictable. Family. Plenty of food. Beauty surrounding them. Marriage to Atu. Children.

Kisi wept along with the others.

Chapter 31

August 5, 1777 – Les Cayes, Saint-Domingue, Island of Hispaniola

SYLVAIN, his wife Jeanne and their two daughters Inez and Louise were enjoying their evening meal. Their dining room was lit by multiple candles. Around the perimeter of the room was a large bureau holding their fine china dishes and silver, a large case for his pistols and muskets, a chest for linen, and a large wooden box holding dolls and other toys for the girls.

The furniture was hand-made by his African carpenters. The wood had been harvested from the local mahogany forests. The reddish-brown wood had a tight grain and was polished to a high sheen. Of all his possessions, Sylvain loved his furniture the most. Though his father had been a farmer in northern France, he was also a skilled carpenter. The field work had kept them very busy, but Sylvain loved nothing more than spending time with his father in their small carpentry shop. He'd learned about the various types of wood and how to work with them.

On one trip to the French coast, he and his father had watched the unloading of a ship from the Caribbean. On the wharf, they walked between rows of tobacco leaves, tightly bundled with a wonderful aroma. There were stacks of bagged rice and sugar as well as countless barrels of rum. Sylvain's father became very excited when he walked up to a stack of wood planking. Piled high on the dock was a type of wood Sylvain had never seen before.

"Look Sylvain, this is the wood that comes from the New World. It's called mahogany. It's used in making the finest musical instruments as well as the most beautiful furniture. It's harder than our oak trees and has a tight grain that helps keep moisture out. The captain's quarters on ships have it lining their walls and floors. It polishes to a very smooth and bright finish. In my opinion, there isn't a better wood anywhere in the world."

Sylvain's curiosity about the New World was piqued on that day at the wharf. Watching the rough seamen unloading the rich bounty of the Caribbean stirred something deep inside of him. It was then he knew he wouldn't work the fields of France his entire life.

Gently nudged back into the present, he listened to the girlish giggles of his two beautiful daughters and watched his lovely Jeanne smiling at them. He knew he was a blessed man.

Standing quietly in the corner of the dining room was a black girl named Liza. She'd been with his family for three years and was likely twenty-years-old. He smiled as he thought of the nickname he'd given her. He liked to call her 'Ghost' because she had the ability to serve them quietly and inconspicuously. She took wonderful care of their needs at the table without being asked and they hardly knew she was there.

Behind him was an African woman named Elsa whom he secretly called 'General'. She was a different story than sweet Liza. Elsa was in her forties and had been serving white people long before his family had arrived in Les Cayes. She had more authority and responsibility than almost any of the other Africans under his control. She was a no-nonsense woman. He sometimes wondered if she'd been a queen in her African village. Both Elsa and Liza were loved by Inez and Louise as their lives intertwined on a daily basis. Their plantation home ran efficiently under the watchful eyes of 'The General'.

He remembered the day, three years earlier, when Liza ascended the platform at the Les Cayes sale barn. He was standing beside Francois, his close friend and boss, as they pondered which of the Africans they'd be buying for the Labreche family plantation.

Watching her closely, he knew this young girl was exactly who he wanted working in his home. He nudged Francois, who followed his gaze as the girl filed past them. That day, they returned to the plantation with another hundred slaves, including the girl.

Bringing her to the house, he introduced Liza to Jeanne, Inez and Louise. They immediately accepted her. Elsa began training her and the rest was history. She was young enough to win the appreciation of his two young girls and she became almost like family.

A year after Liza had arrived in Les Cayes, she became pregnant. Her son was born and named Isaiah. It wasn't long before his light mulatto skin set him apart from most other Africans on the plantation. There were other children with light brown skin who obviously had European fathers. Though Isaiah was different than most other children, he wasn't alone.

Jeanne never talked about it. She'd noticed the extra attention Sylvain gave Liza and Isaiah, but she never asked about it, and of course her husband never shared.

Liza automatically received the benefits which came to the Africans working in the 'big house', but disliked how other slaves would turn their heads when she walked by. She was a slave just like the rest, but other Africans resented her position. She was just as much a captive as the others. She likewise was being exploited and used. It was still slavery, just in a different way. She felt badly at how her fellow Africans were being treated in the fields, but what could she do?

Isaiah was now two-years-old and he played with Inez and Louise like a little brother. Sylvain smiled as he knew Isaiah was just as much family to him as were his girls. He had a son.

Children born of African slave women and fathered by their French masters were born free. They were called mulatto which Francois knew was derived from the Spanish and Portuguese word for 'mule' which was highly derogatory for any African. He knew life wouldn't be easy for his little Isaiah as whites would treat him as African. The presence of African blood in the mulattoes clearly identified them as African, inferior and thus not worthy of the same rights as white men. Though free-born, he'd still be considered African and thus only slightly superior to the slaves.

Again, the giggles of Inez and Louise reminded him of his duty to get the girls ready for bed. He stood and chased them up the wide and winding staircase to their bedroom.

Jumping into the girl's shared bed, they made room for him. He expertly crawled between them. A single candle lit the pages of a small book Sylvain began reading, titled, *The Little Princess*.

His reading soon had them sleeping. Carefully sliding out of bed, he tenderly covered them, leaned down and kissed each one on their forehead. As always, he watched them for a few seconds, said a prayer for them and walked away with the candle in his hand.

Descending the stairs to the first floor he entered the kitchen. Picking up a loaf of bread and bowl of fruit, he walked out the back door. Picking his way on the stone pathway, illuminated by a half moon, he approached Liza's hut. Candlelight from within was escaping through the cracks in the wall. Opening the door, he set the bread and fruit on a wooden bench in the single room hut. Picking up Isaiah, he tickled him and laid him on his woven reed mat. Giving him a kiss on his cheek, he turned his attention to Liza.

~

In the morning Sylvain rode north to the Labreche fields. Already the heat was beginning to pound downward. Prior to lunch he'd meet with each of his twenty-four overseers and their right-hand men. Then he'd head to the mahogany tree to meet with Francois.

He'd never been jealous of Francois' rise to Plantation Manager. His own skills were much more down to earth than those of Francois. He'd always loved working with his hands, so overseeing a thousand field-hands working with their hands, was very satisfying to him. Likewise, he'd always considered Francois more of the upper-class leader type who was a bit more delicate than himself. Sylvain didn't mind following a strong leader. They were definitely different, but complemented each other's styles in a powerful way. Sylvain smiled as he realized their personalities were as different as his own bald head and Francois' full head of red hair.

The Labreche plantation was the largest in the Les Cayes plains. Most plantations had less than a hundred field hands. But the need for more product to supply the growing cities of Europe and England had been doubling over the last decades and the Labreche family had risen to the challenge.

Francois had recently shared some interesting history with Sylvain, who had been amazed at how things were changing. He'd said, *"In the first decade of the 1700's, France built nearly one-hundred sugar cane plantations in Saint-Domingue. The sugar exported to Europe was always increasing. In 1680, there had been only 2,500 slaves in all of Saint-Domingue. By 1700, there were over 10,000 total. Twenty years later, France was bringing in 7,000 more slaves each year to Saint-Domingue.*

"Then, in the 1730's, the French began growing coffee and things were never the same. France was producing two-thirds of the world's coffee by 1750 and the need for more and more slaves has been increasing ever since. There are now almost 500,000 African slaves in Saint-Domingue and our plantation has the most in all of the southwest."

Sylvain realized the heavy responsibility he had in managing 1,000 men and women in the Labreche fields. He knew if he and his overseers weren't careful, the slaves could take advantage of them quickly.

He arrived at the mahogany tree, tied his horse and sat down beside Francois. With his back against the large tree, he settled in for a sandwich with his boss.

Francois asked, "So, is everything in order?"

"Yes. There was trouble in the cane fields this morning but it's been handled."

"What happened?"

"One of the African women went into labor and wouldn't you know it, she had her baby right there in the field. Others stopped their work and we had to get the gawkers back to cutting cane. We sent the woman and child back to her hut. She'll be back to work in a couple of days."

Sylvain continued, "I'm sure I don't need to remind you, but we've lost twenty workers in the last two months. Accidents, runaways and illnesses have taken a toll. When do you think the next ship will be coming?"

"I know the *L'ange D'or* left Guinea ten weeks ago on May 20th. I'd expect it to arrive in a week or so. Captain Jean is bringing 450 Africans but I'm guessing the number will be more like 400 by the time he arrives. How many should we plan on buying?"

"I think another 150 or 200 would do."

"Well, last year, around 15,000 arrived on Saint-Domingue and it looks like the number is increasing every year. With ships arriving every month, we should be able to buy the slaves we need. Prices for Africans are going up, but so are our profits. We're having another phenomenal year. The Labreche family is very pleased."

Chapter 32

August 7, 1777 – On Board the *L'ange D'or* Slave Ship

CAPTAIN Jean thought about his last ten weeks of voyage from the Gold Coast of Africa. Though there'd been the usual number of storms and typical crew issues, he was thankful he'd lost only thirty-two of his precious African cargo so far. It was usually worse. When dysentery would hit his ships in the past, he'd lost anywhere from 100 to 150 Africans and crewmen.

He knew the *L'ange D'or* was only about three days out from docking at the French port of Les Cayes, Saint-Domingue in southwest Hispaniola, so his losses had likely plateaued except for the final culling process.

Completing his records, he stood up from his desk and headed to the main deck. On the way, he asked Pierre to join him at the ships wheel.

Each trip had its good points and bad. One of the great things on this trip for the captain had been Pierre. He'd grown fond of young Pierre and took pride in the mentoring he'd poured into him. He was hoping he could deliver a healthy, bronzed, muscular, well-rounded, sea-worthy young man to his mother Antoinette in Bordeaux. Pierre hadn't disappointed the captain, but the trip wasn't over yet.

At the wheel, the captain called for the first-mate. "We should be sighting Hispaniola in about two days, so we need to get the Africans prepared for the sale. Let's start the culling."

After the first-mate left to fulfill the captain's orders, Pierre said, "I'm surprised we're just two days out."

"If you could see just a little further than the horizon, you'd see Hispaniola over the starboard side. It's about 50 miles from here. We'll stay south of the island to skirt around the pirates who tend to watch for ships that are much closer to shore. They tend to lurk in the bays of Santo Domingo catching French ships sailing into Les Cayes. Their frigates aren't loaded with cargo and have no problem in catching a fully loaded slaver. As we sail further west, we'll cut northwest into our port. Two-thirds of Hispaniola is the eastern Spanish side which is called Santo Domingo. The other third of the island to the west is French Saint-Domingue. So, yes, in about two days you'll see Les Cayes."

"What did you mean when you told the first-mate to begin culling?"

The captain hesitated, realizing that Pierre's values and morality were about to be tested.

He began, "I've mentioned several times how we Europeans are blessed in many ways and are taught to share those gifts with others. One way we do that is to bring our culture, education and experience to others around the world who need to learn from us. We provide a lot of that to the African people, as their pagan lifestyle and backwardness is just waiting for our teaching.

"The Africans on board our ship will soon be adding a lot of value to mankind. Saint-Domingue is called the *Pearl of the Antilles* because of its high profitability and ability to provide resources around the world. These Africans will help this world become a better place. If we didn't help them find their place in the world, they'd simply be living out their lives doing nothing worthwhile in their pagan villages.

"I'm telling you this, hoping you understand how vital it is to bring healthy and strong Africans to the fields. The weak and sickly take a lot of time and money in caring for them and that drops profitability and output. Culling the sick and weak actually makes the rest of them more productive and stronger. Do you understand?"

Pierre paused and said, "I understand what you're saying, but how do you cull them?"

"Well, we'll bring the Africans to the main deck over the next two days to determine their health and strength. The doctor will have a very busy two days. We'll wash, shave and examine all of them. That inspection is what we call 'culling'."

As they'd been talking, the first group of men were brought to the main deck. Pierre watched as the men shielded their eyes from the bright sun. They were lean from the voyage, some were emaciated. One by one, the men were washed, their heads were shaved and the doctor examined them.

He probed and poked, inspecting their muscles. He had them dance a jig to check for coordination and strength. It was obvious the doctor had been through this many times before. When he was finished they were in two groups. One group was very large while the other had only four men.

Crew members grabbed the four men, took them to the gunwale and threw them overboard through an opening in the netting. Pierre gasped. Shocked, he looked at the captain who was watching the process intently. Pierre looked back to the gunwale, halfway expecting to see the Africans still standing there. But it hadn't been an illusion. The four men were gone!

"Pierre, that's the culling process. The weak must die to strengthen the rest. There's no market in Les Cayes for the weak. It's a sad thing, but necessary."

The process continued with more men being examined, a few being thrown overboard, while the rest went back to the lower deck. Pierre wondered how the doctor could live with himself in making these choices. Did he think he was God?

Pierre thought about the atrocities he'd witnessed on his voyage. Girls and women had been abused and tormented. Whippings. Humiliation. The Africans had endured their hell for nearly three months. There had been so many things he'd observed. When he thought he'd seen the worst, something else would happen which was more horrific than the one before. Was the entire crew on board this ship just as guilty as the doctor playing God? His heart was broken and his mind was filled with frustration, anger and confusion.

Then the first group of women and girls arrived on deck. Once again, the humiliating examinations began. Probing, poking and inspecting. Again, as always, the result was two groups, one large and one small. Except this time there was a slight difference.

Within the small group were two healthy young women. The difference was their recognizable pregnancy. They hadn't shown it when they'd been captured or housed at the white building, but after months at the Castle and on board, it became obvious.

~

Kisi stood motionless with fifty other women on the deck. They'd just been shaved by a crewman and inspected by a white man. She recognized the Fante woman, Adzo, whom she'd met at the castle and who was now part of a small group about twenty feet away. Kisi remembered the time four months earlier when Adzo had told her she was pregnant by the white men at the castle. Her stomach was now protruding with evidence of her horrible life at Cape Castle. Their eyes locked in recognition. They smiled at one another.

Suddenly, crewmen grasped the arms of the two pregnant girls and roughly pulled them toward the gunwale. Kisi heard Adzo's startled scream and saw the fear in her eyes as two crewmen grabbed her arms and legs.

~

Pierre stood numbly beside the gunwale with the captain. He watched in horror as the two pregnant women were thrown overboard. Mutely, he looked imploringly at the captain.

Looking over the gunwale, he cringed as they hit the water and was shocked to see them immediately and viciously attacked by sharks tracking the *L'ange D'or.* The water where they landed instantly turned crimson. Pierre vomited over the gunwale.

The captain looked at Pierre and said, "I don't like it either Pierre. But, what else can we do? An obviously pregnant African has very little value at the slave sale. Who would buy her knowing she could die in childbirth? What value could she add if she couldn't work or had to constantly stop to nurse her baby? There's no market for them in Les Cayes. This is all about business. If we'd have known they were pregnant at the Castle, we wouldn't have bought them."

The captain continued, "Pierre, I have something to take care of. If you've seen enough here, come with me. You may as well watch and learn."

He gathered the first, second and third mate along with the doctor and said, "It's time for each of you to quietly identify the African you want for your personal bonus. You can sell him or her in Les Cayes, or you can take them to serve you in France."

The captain gave each of them a numbered brass tag to attach to their African of choice.

~

Atu was surprised to see five white men and the boy entering the hold. Cautiously walking between the Africans, they seemed to be searching for something, or more likely, someone. One of the men stopped by a large man and attached a metal tag to his chain. The others continued their search.

Soon, another two men were tagged. Atu anxiously watched as one of the men visually inspected a man close to him, then moved on. Then, returning, he was standing over Atu, peering in the semi-darkness. Reaching out his hands, he attached a tag to Atu's chain. Atu recoiled as if touched by something hot. What did this mean?

The men left and Atu once again felt fear of the unknown.

~

Quickly, two days went by. The culling process was finished. Pierre had earlier grown accustomed to the many horrible things happening on the voyage. But the last two days were incredibly harder than any storm he'd gone through. In fact, he felt like his mind was in a swirling hurricane. Turmoil. Fear. Torment. It didn't stop.

He heard a crewman atop the main mast hollering and looked up. The man was pointing to his right over the starboard side. Pierre shielded his eyes from the morning glare on the water and got a glimpse of mountains on the horizon.

He stayed on the main deck and continued watching. In the distance he saw another ship sailing east. It was likely returning to England or Europe with their Saint-Domingue cargo as they sailed the last leg of the Atlantic Trade Triangle. He realized it was the first ship they'd seen in three months.

Drawing steadily closer to the island, Pierre felt his pulse quicken. The smell in the fresh air was different than that of the constant Atlantic trade winds. It was pleasant.

The captain pointed and said, "Pierre, if we were closer to shore you'd see an old Spanish fort that the French now use. It's at a village called St. Louis du Sud. The French took it from Spain over 100 years ago. The fort is still active and helps to keep the pirates at bay."

Late in the afternoon they spotted land over the port side. The captain said, "That's another island called *Ile-a-Vache,* or the *Island of Cows*. We'll drop anchor soon in the Les Cayes bay. Tomorrow morning we'll move to the dock and unload our cargo. Les Cayes will be our home for about two weeks. Then we'll head back to Bordeaux and your mother."

Pierre smiled.

Soon the sails were lowered and the ship's anchors dropped. It seemed strange to have the ship motionless in the water. The water in the bay was turquoise. He rested his arms on the starboard gunwale and gazed at the palm trees. There were so many trees lining the shore, he couldn't see beyond them. The captain had told him this was the land of mountains beyond mountains but he couldn't see any from this view. He could see the dock in the distance as well as fishing boats in the bay. He was looking forward to getting on shore.

Chapter 33

PIERRE rose before dawn and readied breakfast for the captain and mates. Going to the main deck, the sun was just beginning its pink ascent into the Caribbean sky. The crew was readying the ship for its short jaunt to the Les Cayes pier.

The anchor chains rattled noisily as they slid into their port holes and the anchors were secured on the bow. Pierre could sense the eagerness of the crew in their anticipation of their shore time. They were ready to get the ship unloaded.

He wondered what the Africans were sensing below. They could hear the rattling of chains and the thud of the anchors. No one was communicating with them about next steps. He couldn't imagine the apprehension and fear they felt not knowing what was next. He knew they'd been horrified when some of their ship mates were being tossed overboard. What could they possibly be thinking? To be sure, their idea of what a white man was, had now been indelibly etched in their minds. And, most certainly that wasn't a good thing.

The hoisted sails caught the Caribbean breeze and the ship began its short trip to the wharf.

Pierre's heart began beating faster as the large ship approached the massive wooden dock. Bumping into place, the ship was tied to huge wooden posts. The gangplank was lowered.

Captain Jean emerged from his quarters and made his way to the starboard side gangplank. He wore a navy blue coat that hung to his knees with gold fringe at the bottom and a frilled white shirt. He had white, knee-length pants and white stockings up to his knees. A large navy blue triangular hat with gold trim topped off the suit. He was truly a gentleman demanding respect and it was obvious the shore men were giving it to him.

Ships from abroad were the livelihood of this colony. The men who captained these ships were the elite and even more importantly, the adventurers of their day. In Europe, they were the ones responsible for bringing wild tales of adventure and exotic products from faraway and mysterious ports.

A carriage being pulled by two beautiful black horses arrived at the dock. Captain Jean climbed into it and disappeared through a gated wall. The crew continued their duties, though Pierre had no idea what was next. He waited.

An hour later, the captain returned and boarded his ship. He told the crew, "We're ready to bring the Africans up to the main deck. They'll all remain at the dock until the shore crew takes them to the sale barn."

Quickly the crew went below and brought up a few Africans at a time. Some of the crew poured a light oil on the men and women and rubbed it in. The African's skin glowed in the sunshine.

The captain told Pierre, "The oil will cover some of the scars and blemishes of the Africans. It makes them look strong and healthy."

Then he smiled and said, "Of course, it also increases their sales value."

~

The hatch covers and stairway doors were opened. Atu blinked from the bright morning sunshine. As a crewman unlocked his chain from the ships wall, Atu crawled from his shelf and stood.

His legs were wobbly but he quickly regained his strength. He followed the man in front of him up the stairway to the main deck. Emerging, he immediately saw palm trees and was reminded of his home in Guinea and the land of the Fante.

He was confused. Where was he? They'd been on the sea for many, many weeks and now he was in a place that looked like home. How could it be? How big was this world they lived in?

He was roughly pushed into a growing crowd of African men and women on the main deck. Crewmen were shouting at them and continued to shove them until they were tightly packed. Soon the main deck was filled with glistening black bodies. Atu felt the now familiar fear welling up within him. He felt the urge to run, but there was nowhere to go. He waited with the rest.

The sun was beating down and he began to sweat, as did his comrades. Then, white men began pushing them to the gangplank. In single file they began leaving the ship.

~

Pierre stood at the gunwale and watched as the long line of Africans slowly walked the pier to their new home – Saint-Domingue on the island of southwest Hispaniola, in the town of Les Cayes.

There were 402 African men, women and children who had survived the three month journey. Pierre had experienced the same journey and storms as they, but in a very different way. He was thankful for his situation, but at the same time feeling very sympathetic for the Africans.

~

Kisi put her feet on dry ground for the first time in three months. Her head was lowered and her eyes looked at the dirt below. It was dry. There was no vomit. No feces. No urine. No slurry sloshing at her feet. The ground looked like the dirt in her village. Her body swayed as her mind continued thinking she was aboard the ship.

Steadily, all the Africans were ushered off the ship and collected in a large group. Slowly, they began their single-file shuffle inland. They went through a large opening in a stone wall and onto a wide path made of large flat rocks inserted in the ground. She wondered if they had been made smooth by the shuffling feet of earlier African slaves.

There were a few huts on both sides of the lane. Suddenly, a large animal pulling a cart passed beside the group. The animal was as big as a bongo antelope, but had long hair on its neck and a long hairy tail. What was this land she was now a part of?

There were dogs running alongside them barking. She'd seen similar animals in Guinea but they'd been wild and dangerous and were always competing for the same meat the villagers needed.

After walking five minutes, they entered a large building. It had a thatched roof, but the sides were open. It reminded her of their communal building in her village and the many feasts the villagers had together.

A white man pulled her by the arm and locked her wrist chain to an eyelet on a wooden beam. The rest of the men, women and children were likewise shackled.

The fear she was experiencing was now an integral part of her life. Rarely over the last four months since she'd been taken captive had she ever felt relaxed. Even when nothing bad was happening, she was enduring the fear of what would transpire next. There was always something new waiting to happen and those new things were never pleasant. The best things that had happened in the last four months were the times she'd been brought to the main deck for sunshine, exercise and washing. Though the cool water had been refreshing, the leering looks of the crewmen, their taunts and laughter was humiliating and hurtful. But, the worst part had been their continual touching and grabbing whenever they had the opportunity.

She sat on the ground and waited. For what? She had no idea but again, she doubted whatever would come next would be pleasant.

The time slowly crept by and she was thankful she was inside the building. She stood to stretch. Distractedly, she looked over the mass of black humanity before her. Though all of these Africans had been fellow travelers for the last three months, rarely did she get a glimpse of all of them at once. She looked for Darifa to no avail.

Suddenly, she gasped, thinking her eyes were playing a trick. Was it Atu? She knew she couldn't yell his name for fear of a brutal blow from a guard. So she watched. It was Atu!

He was standing about one hundred feet away. She watched him intently. It was obvious he was searching the crowd. He rotated to his left, still searching. Another small turn was all that was needed for him to see her. She watched, holding her breath. He again turned slightly, then suddenly he stopped and stared in her direction. She couldn't hear it but she knew he literally gasped and mouthed her name. He could hardly contain himself as their eyes locked. She smiled and suddenly the world was okay... for a moment or two or three. There was no shouting or waving, just distant smiles between a young couple who should have been married four months earlier.

~

Atu had never experienced such relief and joy. Seeing Kisi was the most unexpected thing he could have imagined or hoped for. He knew there were men and women who had died in the white Castle and on board the ship. He likewise had no idea which ship she'd gotten aboard, nor whether they were going to the same destination. The likelihood of them being at the same place at the same time, after four months of horror and terror, was a miracle. He was overjoyed and his smile showed it.

He thought Kisi looked healthy. She certainly looked beautiful even though they were separated by several hundred Africans. They continued to stare at each other. What else could they do? They were shackled to their own part of the huge building and being watched by guards. But, they were both alive!

Hopes and expectations were rising dramatically in both Atu and Kisi's minds and hearts. For many weeks, each had begun their day with hopelessness. Now, each were fearful about letting this tiny spark of hope ignite something they couldn't control.

Chapter 34

August 13, 1777 – Les Cayes, Saint-Domingue, Island of Hispaniola

FRANCOIS ate his breakfast quietly and alone. Dawn was an hour away and the house was quiet. The day would be long and busy. He'd received word yesterday of the arrival of Captain Jean Moise and the *L'ange D'or*.

He'd been notified, as had several other plantation owners and managers that over 400 Africans would be offered for sale today. This of course wasn't a new thing for him as they purchased new slaves almost monthly. Death of his slaves due to illness, injury or punishment took a heavy and predictable toll as did those who ran away. Having kept a record of every slave the Labreche plantation owned, he knew their average work-life span was only about ten years.

Having finished his breakfast, he mounted his waiting white stallion. Trotting the 300' to the home of Sylvain, he waited patiently next to Sylvain's waiting bay horse and the African who tended the mare. Standing under a nearby tree were eight of Sylvain's French overseers.

Sylvain emerged from his home and smiled at his good friend. When the men were mounted, they made the four mile trip to the sale barn near the docks.

Francois was proud of his stallion. The horses on Saint-Domingue were descendants of the magnificent horses brought by the Spaniards during the 16th century. He'd paid dearly for the white stallion but it'd been worth it. The horse was one of his most prized possessions.

Arriving at the sale barn, they noticed the sale platform was already in place and there were small groups of men in the barn and in the yard.

They dismounted and entered the building. Dawn was casting its first rays of sunshine into the barn and highlighting the 400 Africans. Walking through the aisles with Francois, Sylvain commented, "This group is looking really good. Better than most, I'd say."

"I'd agree, but I'm not surprised. This isn't Captain Jean's first voyage." They both laughed.

They emerged from the barn and walked to the auction platform.

"Francois!"

He turned to see who had called out to him.

"Ah, Frederic. My neighbor, it's good to see you. How're things at the Boudet plantation?"

"Overall things are good. As always, we're needing more field hands."

Frederic was the French manager of a large plantation bordering that of Francois. There were times they assisted one another with equipment and even slaves. The adjoining plantations were owned by the Labreche and Boudet families in Paris who knew one another well. Both families had decided years ago to invest in Saint-Domingue. The relationship between the two managers was deep, but when the bidding began for the Africans, their friendship would be put on hold. It was going to be every plantation for itself.

Francois asked, "How many Africans are you hoping to purchase today?"

"About a hundred. I've talked to the other managers this morning and it appears 400 Africans aren't going to be enough to go around. I'm guessing the prices are going to be high."

"Well, at least the ships are coming in more often than in the past. They'll need to step up the flow or we'll be short of field-hands."

Francois laughed, "What? Are you afraid we're going to run out of livestock from Africa?"

Frederic responded with a grin, "Ha. Likely not. They breed like rabbits over there and it's a big continent. I suppose they'll continue to meet our needs."

He continued, "Last month, a rum-soaked slaver captain got a little loose with his talk and told me he was paying $16.00 for a slave at the Gold Coast. Since we're paying about $50.00 for them here, that's quite the markup."

"Yes, I'd agree, but I don't think I'd like the responsibility of trying to get a group of 400 all the way here from Africa."

"You're sure right on that count! Oh, it looks like the sale is about ready to start."

~

Pierre had slept aboard the ship in the harbor and they'd rowed to the shore before dawn. Some of the crew had stayed in the barn overnight guarding the Africans though he wasn't sure why, since they were chained and shackled. But, until they were sold, they were owned by the captain and the ship's owners in France.

Pierre now sat beside the captain just to the side of the three-foot wooden sales platform. He assumed there must be many plantations in the area as he watched the white men coming. They'd been arriving since dawn.

The captain had said they'd explore Les Cayes over the next days after the sale was completed. Pierre was really looking forward to that!

"Captain Jean Moise!"

Looking up, Pierre saw two French gentlemen walking toward them. One had long red hair and the other was bald. The captain stood with a wide grin and said, "My friends, Francois and Sylvain! It's very good to see you again! How are your families?"

"We're all well and really thankful you and your cargo arrived safely. How was your voyage?"

"The voyage was a good one. A few storms but we're here, none worse for the wear."

A man with a long, black frock coat ascended the steps to the platform. Pierre smiled as he knew the man would be sweating profusely in the morning sun.

He said with a booming voice, "Please gentlemen. Please take your seats. We'll begin the sale of the African stock soon."

He proceeded to share the rules of the sale, "All the stock will be sold just as you see them. You may view and inspect the livestock prior to them coming to the platform. The inspection area is directly behind me. Once the stock is on the platform, the bidding will start. It will become your personal property when I point to you and say 'sold'. At that point the new owner has full responsibility to secure the property and take possession. All sales are final and paid with currency, gold or silver."

Twenty Africans entered the inspection area. If Pierre hadn't known better, he'd have thought a cattle sale was about to begin. The wooden corral behind the sales platform even looked like something to hold cows.

He looked at the Africans in the pen. They were oiled and glistening in the morning sunshine. Pierre could almost smell and feel their fear. For certain, he could see it. Their downcast eyes and stooped shoulders almost brought tears to his eyes.

The guard brought the first African man to the platform. His head moved from side to side as if searching for a way to flee. He stopped in the middle of the platform and hung his head.

The African was tall, broad and muscular. Pierre wasn't a plantation manager but he thought this man would be a great worker in the fields. Then, suddenly, he was ashamed at even thinking like a slave-owner.

The sale began and a minute later, after a $55.00 sale, the man was taken off the platform by a white man and led back into the building. An ownership tag was tied securely to the African's iron shackle and he once again was secured to the building.

Pierre looked at the two men who had won the bid. They were the two men the captain had called Sylvain and Francois. They were smiling and seemed pleased with their purchase. Pierre wondered if the African's life was going to improve from what they'd experienced on the ship. Possibly in the next few days he'd be able to learn what life was like on the plantations.

A young girl about his own age came up the steps to the sale block. All alone, head hanging...

The bidding started and again, the sale was finalized at $55.00. The man who had just purchased her was laughing as were the men surrounding him. Pierre wondered why her price was so high, since she sold for the same price as the strong, muscular young man.

She was led off and taken to another vacant area in the building, tagged and shackled.

The sale continued. Pierre asked the captain, "Are you happy with how the sale is going?"

"Yes, the ship's owner will be pleased. You never know for sure what the market price will be until you get here. If disease hits a plantation, the demand for stock rises and so does the price. This is all about supply, demand and of course profit. Today, it appears the prices will be high. That's a good thing for me personally because my share of the profits will be higher."

He continued, "The Spaniards were very busy in the 15th and 16th century in sailing abroad and claiming land on behalf of their Spanish crown. They said it was for the purpose of sharing the Church and God with the heathen. However, most countries felt the Spaniards were only after gold and trade. In reality Pierre, maybe the money is what drives this Atlantic Trade Triangle and all of us."

~

Two hours later, Kisi watched as the guards came into her section of the barn and began releasing twenty girls and women. She was herded into the group.

She was driven into the fenced corral. Standing with the other women, they were soon joined by ten men who began their inspections. She felt like an animal. She was feeling humiliation yet again, and of course, the ever-present fear.

The first girl was led to the auction block and sold. Then the next girl followed. Then it was Kisi's turn. As she was led up the steps, she noticed the young white boy from the ship sitting with the captain. Their eyes met for an instant and then she was on the platform.

Quickly her sale was over. The seller had pointed to a red-haired man in the front row who smiled. Then she was led back to the barn and chained in place. A tag was placed on her shackle and it was done.

~

The sale continued. Pierre asked the captain what the doctor and mates would be doing with their bonus slaves. The captain told him that three of the four had decided to take their Africans back to France. Having a black servant in their home would be a huge blessing and their social status would be elevated. Their wives would have less work to do.

The third-mate's African was still in the barn. His life was different than that of the doctor and the other mates. He wasn't married and would likely continue his sea voyages with the captain, so he chose to sell his young African here in Les Cayes.

As the sale continued, the third-mate's young African who was about Pierre's age was brought to the sales platform. The bidding began and when it was over, the hammer fell at $60.00. The losing bidder, the man with red hair, nodded at the winning bidder, his friend and neighbor, Frederic. The third-mate was pleased.

The sale soon ended. Francois and Sylvain gathered their nine helpers and went to the sale barn. Their 143 Africans were unshackled from the barn, then chained together for the four mile walk to their new home on the Labreche plantation.

Frederic and his 105 Africans began their four mile trek to the Boudet property.

Pierre watched as all of the *L'ange D'or* Africans shuffled to their unknown futures. He continued observing as the various plantation managers departed with their stock. Some of the groups were small and some were large. The red-haired man with his bald friend were leading the largest. The smallest was a group of three women. There were fourteen groups going in various directions to different plantations, but all for the same reason. These Africans would be the men and women who made Saint-Domingue the Pearl of the Antilles. They were the ones whose long hours and short lives produced the products making Saint-Domingue the richest colony in the New World.

Chapter 35

THEY sat quietly in the open aired building, four days after the sale and were thankful for the Caribbean air gently swirling through. Pierre watched Francois' red hair flutter in the breeze. Beside Francois was his wife and their two boys. There were over sixty white men, women and children attending the Sunday Mass.

The priest had delivered a liturgy to the group. Pierre pondered the various things he'd heard. Primarily the priest had focused on St. Matthew 7:12 which was about, *'Doing to others what you'd want them to do to you'.*

The church service on the Labreche plantation ended. The priest introduced himself and moved on. Captain Jean had been invited to the plantation and chose to bring Pierre with him. Soon, they'd be touring the Labreche property and then enjoying a Sunday afternoon dinner with the family.

Emerging from the church service, Pierre stopped and admired the surroundings. The numerous white buildings were large and scattered over many acres. The green, lush grass was neatly trimmed and there were huge amounts of waving palm trees, beautiful flowers and shrubs.

The captain interrupted his musings and said, "Pierre, it's time for a carriage ride."

Pierre joined the captain, Francois, his wife and their boys in the large carriage. Within five minutes they stopped beside a huge cotton field next to a large but nearly dry river. The large green plants in the field were loaded with white cotton bolls. African slaves were busy picking the cotton and dropping the bolls into woven wicker baskets made from palm fronds.

Pierre looked at Francois and asked, "Do the Africans need to work on Sunday?"

"Yes, they work every day. They don't have any holy days since they are pagan. They just don't seem to comprehend much about the Church and God."

They continued their carriage ride to the end of the field and came to a large building. Inside were women and children tediously going through the cotton bolls and removing the stray leaves, sticks and seeds. The cleaned cotton was piled in huge bins. In another area of the building, Francois showed them the large bales of cotton ready for shipment to Europe.

Back in the carriage they soon arrived at a large field of sugar cane. Pierre observed many slaves cutting and trimming the stalks. Others were throwing the unused leaves and brush into a large pile that would eventually be burned.

A large wagon was being loaded with the cane stalks. As Pierre looked around, he saw mountains to the north and west but here before him were a few miles of utterly flat plains filled with a variety of crops.

After a five minute carriage ride they entered another large compound. He stood in awe as he looked at the massive stone pillars, walls and buildings.

Francois said, "This is where the sugar cane is processed. The wagons bring it into the mill area. Water is flushed into the mill from the river through underground tunnels made from rock as well as above ground sluices. The cane stalks are pushed under the large mill stone to crush them. The water carries the juices and liquids to the cooking area.

There, Pierre saw large copper kettles being heated with charcoal. The juices were being boiled and the water evaporated as steam leaving a residue in the kettle. The residue was poured into large flat pans and allowed to crystallize into sugar.

In one of the large stone depots, there were dozens of large bags of crystallized sugar ready to export to Europe and England. Francois scooped up a handful of sugar and offered a taste to Pierre. Pierre squeezed some between his thumb and finger and dropped it on his tongue. This was the first raw sugar he'd ever tasted and it was incredibly sweet. He smiled. Francois picked up a small bag and filled it with sugar, tied it off and gave it to Pierre.

The afternoon quickly went by and they returned to Francois' home for their dinner. Behind their home was a large courtyard shaded by palms, fir and mango trees. The ground of the courtyard was covered in flat stones, laid in beautiful and intricate patterns. In the middle was a large table of food. Pierre had never seen so much food at one time in one place.

Stepping up to the table he saw chicken, pork, beef and platters of vegetables and fruit. There was bread still warm from the oven, along with a plate of hard candies.

Sylvain and his family arrived, so Francois invited his guests to the table. When all were seated, Francois asked the captain to offer thanksgiving for the meal.

"Thank you Father for the food we're about to eat. You bless us abundantly in every way and every day and we say thanks. We pray that we can do as the priest instructed us this morning, to treat others like we'd want them to treat us. We're thankful that together we can be a part of helping the poor Africans find a better and more fulfilled life than what they had in Africa. Amen."

The food was passed and the conversation turned to many subjects. Then Francois asked, "Pierre, I have a question for you. How was your experience on the ship?" All eyes were on Pierre.

Hesitating, he said, "Well, it was an education, just like the captain said it'd be."

"How so?"

Again hesitating, he said, "My life in France was very sheltered, as it was just my mother and I living in a very small home. My life was filled with going to school and making sure my mother and I were able to put food on our table and pay our bills. So, being on a ship and seeing all I've seen is very new to me. It's been an education."

Francois pressed, "Would you say it's been a good education?"

"I think learning new things is always good. Some of what I've learned has been difficult. What I've learned will change my life."

"So, how was it that you became a seafaring sailor at your young age?"

Pierre looked at Captain Jean who simply said, "Pierre's mother became a widow. Her husband had been on my ship and lost his life so she was in dire straits. We agreed that Pierre should join this voyage to earn wages to help them survive."

Francois asked Pierre, "You've seen a lot since you've landed in Les Cayes. Do you have any questions?"

Pierre looked at the captain who nodded encouragement to him. "I probably have a hundred questions. Listening to the priest this morning made me think about a question I've been wondering about."

"Go ahead, lad."

"Well, the priest was talking about what the Bible said in St. Matthew about treating others like we'd want to be treated. The captain mentioned it also in his prayer. My question is this. I've watched how the Africans were treated at the Cape Coast Castle in Guinea, on board the ship, at the slave sale and now on the plantations. I know I wouldn't want to be treated like they've been treated, so why is it okay to treat other human beings in a way we wouldn't want to be treated?"

Everyone around the table grew quiet, so Pierre looked around to see if anyone had heard his question.

Francois answered, "That's certainly not the first time I've heard this question and I've had to settle it in my own mind as well. Let me see if I can help you understand.

"Over the years I've talked to many captains who've brought Africans to Les Cayes. They tell us what they've learned about the African life. No longer can Europeans send their white men into the jungles of Africa to find people to bring to the New World. Many white men have lost their lives to pagan, wild tribes who have even ate the Europeans. That's how the Africans treat others. We have the Biblical right and authority to treat them as they treat us.

"Some of the Africans we buy at the Gold Coast were already slaves to other tribes before being sold to us. Slavery isn't new in Africa. They've been doing it for centuries and are still doing it. We're not doing anything different to them than they already do to each other, or what they'd do to us if they captured us. Our goal is to bring them to a place where they can learn the French language and about our God. By watching our example they can begin to develop their own land and start businesses. Their countries need to be brought into the 18th century."

Pierre said, "Thanks. I didn't know most of that history about Africa." Pausing to collect his thoughts, he continued, "But, I thought the Bible said we should treat others like we wanted to be treated. It seems what you described is about treating others like they treat us? That seems different. All I know is I don't want to be treated like they're being treated. What would happen if we treated them like human beings, instead of livestock?"

Everyone at the table was still quiet when the captain spoke, "Pierre, I've been where you're at. Those are questions without answers. Over the years, I've learned much. I trust most of what I've learned is wisdom rather than folly. As you get older and better understand the ways of the world, you'll likely see things differently. God has obviously blessed the white people with better education, more intelligence and business minds. Since we're superior, the Bible tells us to be good stewards of what God's given us. We're taught to not bury our talents in the ground but to use them. I think what you've seen on the plantation today would be proof that we're fulfilling God's will and plan."

Francois quickly said, "Well, enough of the heavy, intellectual philosophy. Let's have some of that dessert and candy!"

~

The next day, the captain was busy laying the groundwork for purchasing cotton, tobacco, sugar, rum, royal blue indigo ink, coffee, mahogany and other items to supply the growing European markets. The next week he'd have all the purchasing completed and the crew would be getting the ship loaded for departure.

Pierre stayed aboard the ship during the week scrubbing and washing, along with countless other duties in preparation for the six week journey home.

By the end of the week, Pierre was proud of how clean the ship had become again. During the slave voyage, it had become incredibly filthy. Cleaning the lower decks had been a horrible job and seemed to take forever, but they'd got it done. All that time below decks, he'd felt a connection to the men and women who had occupied the cramped spaces for nearly three months.

He was getting excited to see his mother again.

Chapter 36

August 22, 1777 – Labreche Plantation – Les Cayes, Saint-Domingue

KISI laid quietly in a hut. The moon was casting shadows and a bit of light into her new home which she shared with ten other girls and women. Above her was palm leaf thatching. Surrounding her was a wall made of dried mud and dung. On the floor was a woven palm frond mat separating her from the rich Hispaniola soil.

She listened to the night noises surrounding her. She'd been amazed to learn that half of the women spoke Fante. Though their villages had been far apart, they had a common language and culture. Each had a story to tell.

One of the girls had been married almost two years ago in northeast Guinea. She and her husband then had a small son. One afternoon when working alone in one of the village's gardens, she'd been abducted by strangers. No one had seen the kidnapping. She wept as she told her sad story, wondering what her son and husband were doing without her.

A sweet young girl of twelve told her story of being alone in her village taking care of two babies. Their mothers and the others were working in the fields. Suddenly, men came into the village. Being alone, she hid in one of the huts with the babies. Then one began crying and the door flap flew open. The babies were left crying in the dirt as she was taken. She cried as she wondered what her mother and father thought when she was suddenly gone.

Another girl had been betrothed and married to a man from another village. He had become dissatisfied with his new bride and chose to sell her to foreign traders coming through their region heading to the coast.

The stories went on and on. Kisi shared her story of betrothal, capture and journey to the sale barn. Some of the women cried with her.

One of the girls asked, "What's happened to your fiancé Atu?"

"I saw him going to the sale platform but I didn't see him after that. I only know he didn't come with our group to this plantation. At least I know he's alive and healthy. But I don't know if I'll ever see him again since we're both slaves on different plantations."

One of the older women in the hut said, "Never give up hope. I think that's all we have left."

Listening to the soft sounds of the girls sleeping in the hut, Kisi reflected on the days since she'd been sold at the barn. The day following the sale, she and others had walked to a large field. She'd spent a long, hot day picking cotton. The next day was spent in cutting the leaves from the plants which produced the blue indigo ink.

The third day she picked cotton seeds from the cotton. On the fourth day she'd kept the fires burning under the large copper pots boiling the sugarcane syrup to produce sugar.

She knew she was being watched. It seemed the overseer was trying to determine where she'd be best used. Then the next day she was back in the big building removing cotton seeds from the bolls. She thought this might be her new work. She was thankful for the shade of the building and the opportunity to sit, but had sympathy for the girls and women working in the hot sun picking the cotton.

She knew she needed to do her job well or she'd likely find herself tending a boiling, sugar-making pot in the hot Caribbean sun. She didn't want that. If she was going to survive, she knew she'd have to be smart.

The tears came once again as she thought of her mother and father. She missed them and Atu. She missed Darifa. She thought about how pregnant Adzo had been tossed like garbage over the ship's rail. Then, crying softly, Kisi fell asleep.

~

Atu had never been so exhausted in his entire life. His African tribal years hadn't been easy, but it was nothing compared to this work. For the past week, he'd been up at dawn and back in his hut at dusk. They were long, hard and hot days.

He'd worked in the sugar cane fields for days on end. Cutting, cutting, cutting the endless rows of stalks which were much taller than he was. He was no stranger to a machete. They'd used them in Guinea to clear the jungle as well as harvesting their crops. Though difficult and never-ending, his job was easier than constantly lifting the heavy bundles of cane onto the large carts and wagons. It'd only been a week and already he was wondering what it'd be like to use his machete to catch his guard unaware and escape.

He enjoyed the quiet hut time after dark. The work was done, their meager meal had been eaten and there was time to talk. On board the ship and in the Cape Coast Castle, there was little opportunity to find someone who knew Fante. Now he was living in a small hut with eight men. Five of them were Fante and he was learning a lot about their individual lives. Not only did they share their stories about their personal kidnapping, but they shared what they remembered of others they'd talked to in the last months. History was always being made and was now being passed on to others.

Two of the men in his hut had been caught stealing from another village in Africa. They were caught and kept as slaves until the slave-traders came to their region. Then they were sold. Their tragic stories regarding the trek through the desert and jungles of Africa, the white Castle and the journey to Hispaniola seemed to be the same as his own. But each of their abduction stories were unique.

One evening, one of the men asked, "What happened to the girl you were engaged to?"

"We saw each other in the sale barn before the sale. I couldn't believe it, because before that I didn't know if she was alive or already dead. I didn't know which ship she got on in Africa, so I had no idea where she'd be taken even if she were alive. Then I saw her a week ago and watched her go to the sale platform. She was bought by a red-haired man who bought many slaves. I have no idea where she is now or if I'll ever see her again."

~

The next morning Atu was busy cutting the cane in the field, but in the afternoon he'd been told to get up on the cart. There he stacked the bundles thrown up to him. While on the cart he had the opportunity to see above the cane and he couldn't believe how huge the cane field was.

The field was endless! He thought his work would never be finished. He also saw green mountains in the distance which stretched across the horizon. The view was spectacular. A flock of white birds flew over the field and he was reminded of home. Atu was mesmerized gazing at the mountains and endless sugarcane. Looking to the west, he saw yet more cane.

His exploring gaze had been abruptly interrupted by the crack of a whip and a brutal lash on his back. Quickly he lowered his head, grabbed a bundle of cane and returned to work but the white man was relentless. He had a point to make and pulled Atu from the wagon by a leg. He fell heavily to the ground where the French overseer whipped him three more times. Scrambling up to the wagon, Atu continued his work.

That evening, a man in his hut washed the blood-caked gashes on Atu's back. He'd said, "I saw you looking across the field and saw the white man on his horse come up behind you. I knew what would happen. I think now, we've all met his whip."

Atu said, "I've seen others get lashed and decided to be careful so it wouldn't happen to me. Now I know I'll need to be even more careful in the future." He'd been amazed how quietly the horse and man had arrived on the scene. It seemed the overseer and his helpers had eyes everywhere.

~

Captain Jean had earlier finished his purchase of cargo to take back to Bordeaux, France. There wasn't a shortage of products to buy, and the sale of the Africans yielded a high profit with which to purchase what he needed. The Atlantic Trade Triangle was truly a well-oiled and smoothly operating machine. Money in and lots of money out. Cargo purchased and cargo sold. Now the Hispaniola products were being loaded and stored aboard the *L'ange D'or*.

He and Pierre now had time to spend two more days touring the Labreche plantation as well as the neighboring Boudet plantation. Francois and Frederic were wonderful hosts and tour guides. On one of those days they ventured further north. They stood on the bank of a large river.

Standing thirty feet above the river bed, Pierre looked down and was amazed. He'd never seen a river like this in France. The river was almost dry with small creeks of water flowing in channels through the rocky maze.

Francois said, "This is Ravine du Sud and we rely on it to bring the water we need for our plantations. When the rains begin in the mountains you see to the north, the water flash floods through this river to the sea. It'll fill this 500' wide river to nearly the brim but will disappear within a couple of days to the Caribbean. When it floods, we bring many of our slaves here to fill the stone aqueducts and cisterns with water which then flows to both our plantation and the Boudet plantation beside us. The land you're standing on is Labreche plantation property. We're fortunate to be right on the river."

Continuing, he said, "As you can see, we never run out of rocks for construction here in Les Cayes. The river provides all the rocks we need, as does the land. We have men and women digging and hauling rocks from the land every day. The rocks aren't a cash crop but a necessary evil we have to deal with. They're put to good use."

As they continued north that day, they arrived at a spectacular waterfall. The water was turquoise and clear. Pierre could see fish swimming in the pool which was surrounded by palms and ferns. Pierre was fascinated by the beauty.

Francois' sons, Dominic and Louis peeled off their clothing and began climbing the cliff beside the waterfall. Pierre watched as they launched themselves into the blue pool beneath them. The captain said, "Go ahead Pierre, you'll likely never have this chance again."

Quickly, Pierre joined the boys.

After a few jumps, he sat at the top of the falls and looked around. Since arriving in Saint-Domingue, it seemed he'd found paradise. He'd seen lush vegetation, large flocks of white cow-birds, parrots, palm trees, pines, wild flowers, wildlife, huge forests of trees, beautiful beaches with turquoise tidal basins, this waterfall and never-ending beauty. It was impossible to take in the magnificence of Saint-Domingue. But, once again, the shadow of the African's plight pushed into his mind. The guilt and shame returned once again.

On the return to their ship, they traveled the lane between the Labreche and Boudet plantations. As far as he could see, he watched the hundreds of African slaves working in the fields as if their lives depended on it, and he was sure that was the case. The Africans were everywhere in the Les Cayes plains. He shuddered as he thought of the contrast of his life to theirs. He reminisced about what he'd just seen of this beautiful country which they'd never see or enjoy. Then he thought about how he'd soon return to his own country and his mother once again. These Africans would never see their country or families again.

This country was such a land of contrasts. The difference was stark and literally black and white.

Arriving at the dock in Les Cayes, the first-mate told the captain that the ship was loaded and ready to depart when he was ready. After verifying that the manifest for the cargo had been completed, they climbed into a wooden dinghy and went the short distance to the *L'ange D'or* in the harbor.

Soon, the sails were catching a breeze and the anchors had been secured. Pierre stood at the port side with his elbows leaning on the gunwale. He watched as the dock became smaller and smaller. He had his last glimpse of Caribbean beach as they sailed easterly. They emerged into the open sea east of Hispaniola and he knew he was six weeks from seeing his mother.

He wondered if he'd ever see this place again.

Chapter 37

October 4, 1777 – Boudet Plantation – Les Cayes, Saint-Domingue

ATU was cutting sugar cane. It'd been over two months that he'd been cutting the tall green stalks. Every day. Dawn to dusk. The strength he'd lost on board the ship had now returned. He was physically feeling strong again.

However, the emotional side of him felt weaker. His inability to be with or save his fiancé Kisi tore at his soul, heart and mind. Every day, every hour he thought about her and wondered what she was enduring. He feared for her life. Then he'd remind himself, she was Fante. She was strong and would survive, yet there was always a lingering question. How long could either of them survive in this environment? He'd already seen several men and women die from injury, sickness and disease.

One of the men in his hut had fallen into the sluice of water that fed the mill wheel for crushing sugar cane. In Atu's emotional low times, he'd think the man was the fortunate one. Then he'd stop himself from those kinds of negative thoughts. However, he did wonder if the man fell or if he chose a quick escape from this hell. Who would know for sure? But, one thing was certain, there would always be another African to take his place.

By now the cutting of the cane stalks with his machete was so automatic he didn't have to concentrate. He'd had months to perfect his skills. As he threw the stalks to the ground for the next man to gather and throw onto the wagon, he noticed his pile was growing. He looked around and didn't see the man anywhere.

The French overseer saw the pile of cane growing and rode up to Atu. Atu stood there with his head hanging and the white man knew immediately what was happening. He quickly rode away in a gallop. Within two minutes, he along with four other white men arrived with five large, chained dogs. They looked ferocious and Atu automatically took a step back and kept the machete in front of him.

Holding the dog's noses to the ground where the pile had grown, the dogs quickly got the scent of the missing African. Unleashing the dogs, they tore into the tall sugar cane. Atu kept cutting but trembled as he thought about what would soon happen in the field. The ferocious barking continued. It became even more intense. Then he heard a scream from somewhere in the field. The vicious growling of the dogs as well as the horrible screaming could be heard by everyone within earshot. Then, the screaming abruptly stopped. Ten minutes later the dogs returned to the guards with blood covered muzzles.

Atu continued working. He knew in the next few days, they'd find the decaying remains of yet another mutilated African who risked his life to escape his own personal torment.

The guard quickly brought another slave to gather the cut cane. Plantation life was back to normal. Normal. Atu knew as long as he'd have life and strength, he'd find a way to claim his bride, even if it took twenty years. He was learning his lessons well.

What could he do to escape? How could he find Kisi? Was it destiny for them to be together?

That evening, Atu thought about the African running into the cane fields, being attacked, killed and likely eaten by the dogs. Sitting with his fellow slaves, he decided to trust the men in his hut and asked the question, "Does anyone ever escape from here?"

Another man said quietly, "That's not something that should be talked about. There are ears everywhere."

Not ready to let it go, he asked again.

A quiet voice said, "Yes. I've been here for six years and I know of maybe twenty men who've gotten away from this plantation. There are rumors the runaways live together in the mountains to the north."

Atu remembered seeing those mountains and they didn't seem too far away. He remembered they were covered in green so he thought it was likely forested.

Hesitating, Atu said, "Tell me what you've learned."

The man, with a hushed voice, continued, "Those runaway Africans are called Maroons. I've learned much of the French men's language and I hear them talking sometimes. They seem to be afraid to go into the mountains, as the Africans know better than anyone how to survive there. The French like to live an easy life and the Africans in the mountains are a strong, dangerous and angry group. They hate the French and continually come down to the many plantations in the plains to raid and steal from them. They're driven by anger and a strong desire to hurt the French."

"How did they escape from their plantations?"

The man said, "I think you may be a young and foolish man with all your questions and dreams. You saw what happened today with the man who tried? There's no way to escape from our huts. It has to be through the fields and the cane is the only crop tall enough to hide in. You have to pick the right time of day and find a way to hide from the dogs. The most important thing is being able to run like the wind and overcome your fear of what's behind you. You have to want what's ahead more than fear what's behind."

"Have you tried to get away?"

"No. I was always too afraid of the whip or the dogs. Now, my strength isn't what it was when I was young. I'd not make it to the mountains."

The hut grew quiet and the men laid on their mats. Soon the sounds of men sleeping grew louder. Atu began thinking of his young life in Africa. His stealth, ability to hide, the patience he'd had in waiting for the bongo and other animals along with his determination, gave him hope. For now, his biggest fear was getting older, weaker and complacent. He didn't want that regret.

It wasn't the mountains that drew him, nor even freedom. Those two things would've been enough under other circumstances, but with him, there was more. Freedom could be the avenue by which he could somehow, someway be with his fiancé. Being with Kisi again was his driving and primary focus. Love was a huge motivator.

He pondered his two biggest questions. When was the best time of the day or night to escape? How can I evade the dogs?

Chapter 38

October 20, 1777 – Bordeaux, France

PIERRE'S heart was beating faster and faster. Two days ago, they'd rounded the northwest tip of Spain into the Bay of Biscay. Now, they'd just entered River Dordogne and took the starboard turn up the Garonne River. On both sides he saw the factories belching their productive black and grey smoke into the blue afternoon sky.

He was thinking about these factories differently than when he'd passed them six months ago. He knew the indigo ink below would soon be dyeing the white textiles in the mills to royal blue. The men in the factories would be smoking the Hispaniola tobacco. Parents would be sharing candies with their children and explaining that the sugar came from Les Cayes, Saint-Domingue.

Most of the products would soon leave the Bordeaux harbor via rivers and roads to the rest of Europe. Bordeaux was only second to London in the number of ships sailing to the Americas, the Caribbean and Central America. Those ships would be making the grand triangular circuit to Africa, the slave ports to the west and then back northeast to France.

He knew word would travel fast that the *L'ange D'or* was arriving and he was hoping his mother would hear about it before he set foot on land.

Quickly walking the main deck to the bow, he looked forward. He saw many ships in the harbor waiting to load cargo while others were unloading or heading to the high seas.

The trip back from Hispaniola was without incident with the exception of one storm, but he'd been through worse. With no Africans to care for, the voyage was pleasant enough.

The captain was skillfully steering the ship into the harbor toward the waiting wharf. A slight bump was all he felt as the ship finally came to rest at its home port. And then, the six month trip was over.

He looked back to the helm and saw the captain smile at him. Then he raised his arm and saluted Pierre. After all these many months at sea and the wide range of experiences, Pierre knew he'd miss the captain and the *L'ange D'or*. He wondered if he'd ever be satisfied in keeping his legs on land. Would the smell of the salty air and the Caribbean sunshine beckon once again?

There were many questions about his future, but one thing was certain. His life would never be the same. He'd changed dramatically. He'd left as a fifteen-year-old boy and returned a sixteen-year-old man.

Six months ago he'd had few opinions and experiences to draw from. He had the privilege of a godly mother full of values, but he'd had few life experiences to put them into practice. Now, he returned with something few young men his age had the opportunity to experience – six months on the high seas with exotic ports of call he couldn't have imagined. He'd missed months of school but had received an education few men at the end of their lives would only have dreamed about.

Then, she was there. Waving! Smiling! Tears flowing down her cheeks. He waved and smiled but checked his tears. He'd be patient and wouldn't show his boyish enthusiasm. The gangplank was lowered. Men began their descent to their families and friends. The ship was now empty of human cargo except for two men. The captain stood by the gangplank and motioned for Pierre to join him. Together they walked down the planks. Antoinette wrapped her arms around her son. Then, holding him at arm's length, she looked up at his bronzed un-freckled face. His hair was long over his ears and neck. His arms were thick and strong. His waist was lean and his chest was wide. She raised her hand and a finger traced the long scar on his forehead.

She said, "Pierre, you look like your father. The sea was good to you." Then they hugged each other.

The captain watched. Antoinette went to him. He stuck out his hand which she pushed away as she hugged him tightly. "Thank you for bringing my son back home safely."

The captain was touched. Pausing he said, "Your son is someone for you to be proud of. I'm sure he'll have much to tell you. I told you I'd give him an education and I think that's been accomplished. I'm not sure what his future holds, but I know it'll be good."

He continued, "May I walk you both to your home?"

"Yes, yes, of course. It's not much but it's still mine, thanks to you. I was angry when you wouldn't pay my husband's wages, but I realized he hadn't fulfilled his contract with you. I also was horrified to see my only son leave, but he's back and better than ever."

Arriving at the small home, they entered. Antoinette heated water and prepared tea. She served a few biscuits as they sat in the small room together. Pierre's body still seemed to be swaying with the waves. He wondered when the motion would leave. Maybe it'd never leave, and he'd keep his memories of the voyage.

Captain Jean said, "Antoinette, six months ago I told you Pierre's service with me on the voyage would pay off the loan I had given you before we left. I want you to know the loan is now paid."

"Thank you for making it possible for me to keep my home. Pierre and I are grateful."

He continued, "However, I've provided him with the education of a lifetime on board ship. How will you pay me for that?"

After an awkward silence, he laughed and said, "I was jesting, Madame. Your son has become a friend and I hadn't expected that to happen. He's a fine young man with morals and opinions different than my own. His innocent questions have caused me to reconsider some of my own sentiments. I've forgotten some of the beliefs I had from many years ago. Pierre's questions and comments brought some of them back. It's been a privilege to serve alongside your son. He's a fine man."

Pierre's cheeks flushed in spite of his bronzed face.

The captain said, "The work he did for me was very helpful. I want to pay him a sailor's wages for what he's done for the *L'ange D'or*. I hope it serves his education and future well."

He handed Pierre a stack of currency with a statement, "Pierre, the only thing I want from you is that you'll stay in touch. I'll give you my address in Paris. Someday when I'm an old man, possibly you can come entertain me with wild tales of your life!"

The captain again reached inside his vest pocket and placed another stack of currency on the small wooden table. "Madame, I've decided to give you the wages your husband would have made had he finished his trip with me. Your son has caused me to reflect on my life and has triggered some emotions in this old sea-salt. I trust your life will be blessed."

They laughed together and the captain disappeared down the path to the harbor.

The door to the tiny home in Bordeaux closed and a mother and son embraced.

~

The next day Pierre and his mother talked for hours on end about his experiences over the last six months. She was just as anxious for his words, as he was in sharing them.

She loved his explanations of Saint-Domingue. She'd had no idea any place on earth existed such as he described. She said, "Pierre, it almost sounds like you're describing Heaven itself!"

She cried when he shared his experiences in Africa on the Gold Coast and how Africans were being torn from their families and friends.

When he finally had answered all her questions and he thought of nothing else, they both grew quiet.

Antoinette asked, "Pierre, I have one more question."

"Yes?"

She hesitated for a few seconds, "Has all of this changed you?"

He lowered his head for two minutes and his shoulders shook as he began crying. She put her arm around him and waited.

Finally he answered, "I'm really angry."

She waited for more.

"I've seen so much evil. How can God let this slavery and horror happen to the African people? It makes me even question if there's a God."

She said, "People have a very difficult time with that very question. I know it's not a new question."

"So, who has the answer?"

She paused, "I think only God can answer that question. He definitely gives us hints in the Bible to help us understand."

"Like what?"

She got her worn and well-marked Bible and opened to 2 Peter chapter 3:9 and said, "It says here that God doesn't want anyone to perish but that all of us need to change our path and follow Him."

Turning further she said, "In Ezekiel 33, He says that He takes no pleasure in the death of the wicked and that we should turn away from all of our wicked ways."

Continuing, "Here in Mark chapter 8 Jesus said if we want to be a follower of Him, we have to deny ourselves, pick up our crosses and follow after Him. In other words, we have to make a choice. We either follow Him or we follow the things of this world."

"In 1 Timothy chapter 2 it says it's God's desire that all men would be saved and come to the truth."

"Pierre, I don't have all the answers, but I know for a certainty that God has given all of us an opportunity to make a choice. But, our choices always impact other people. God doesn't force Himself on us, he wants us to choose Him and His good path. If we choose evil, we'll hurt others. If we choose good things, we can help others. But, make no mistake, there's no evil with God. Any evil you see hasn't come from Him. The Bible says that He is love."

She continued, "Evil, wicked men and their choices will be dealt with. If not now, there'll be judgment before God. One thing's certain, evil will be dealt with."

Pierre looked at his mother and said, "I suppose I'm at a crossroad. I've been given experiences few people have had. My anger is probably directed at choices other people make, rather than toward God. It's difficult for me to be angry with Captain Jean, but he most certainly has been sucked into some wicked things."

She smiled and said, "All of us are responsible for our own decisions. We all must accept God's judgment on our actions in life. You can't take responsibility for Captain Jean's choices or anyone else's for that matter. There's only two questions for you to answer. What are you going to do with your life? What are you going to do about the injustices you've seen?"

"On the return voyage from Hispaniola, I did a lot of thinking. Part of me wanted to be on the high seas visiting exotic places. Another part of me wants to help the Africans. I've wondered about going to seminary to become a Protestant preacher. I'm not sure where that thought came from, but it hasn't left my mind."

Antoinette smiled once again, "Pierre, let's get you through secondary school and then think about your next steps. I'm sure if you're a praying young man, God will direct your path."

Chapter 39

December 18, 1777 – Labreche Plantation – Les Cayes

KISI was the best cotton seed picker on the Labreche plantation. She knew she had to be quiet and do excellent work. If she continued doing that, she could likely keep doing what she was doing. Though difficult, it was certainly easier than any other job she'd seen.

If there was any hope for her and Atu to see one another again, she had to survive. If there was a chance for marriage... she stopped herself. She didn't want her mind lingering too long on hope, as it all seemed so impossible.

She'd met Fante women on the plantation who'd been slaves for over ten years. It was hard to believe the slavery trade had been going on for so long and she'd known nothing about it. She realized she and Atu had been the first ones abducted from their village, so what would the villagers in Africa know? She likewise knew her father would have gone back and told everyone what had happened to her and Atu, so now at least they were warned. She hoped no one would ever experience what she'd been through.

The women who had been here longest were frail, thin and weak, but not old. She was afraid soon she'd become like them.

The best thing that had happened to her in the last months had happened just the day before. She'd been picking the cotton seeds from the bolls as usual when a group of women from the fields brought in their baskets. Not looking up, she heard some quiet talking among the women. Suddenly, she caught her breath as she recognized a voice. She cautiously turned and saw Darifa! Their eyes met! They were on the same plantation! Then Darifa left with the other women for the fields. Kisi's life suddenly became better.

Her job was monotonous. She could perform it without thinking, which gave her ample time to reflect on other things. Most of the days were just like the days before and she liked that. If something out of the ordinary happened, it was never a good thing.

As she was thinking about Darifa being on the same plantation, her thoughts were interrupted by a scream. Turning, she saw white guards outside the building whipping a man. One of the guards came into the building and motioned for the women to follow him.

They stood together in the yard. One of the guards went to each of the women and forced them to raise their heads so they could watch what was happening. When Kisi turned her head to the side, he slapped her and forced her head forward. She obeyed.

The whipping continued. Suddenly two men on horses galloped into the yard. They were the red-haired boss and bald-headed man who had purchased her at the sale.

Dismounting, the bald man stopped the guard from continuing. He walked around the bloodied African lying on the ground and said something to another guard who turned and walked into the cotton field. Soon he brought back two African men.

The guard gave shovels to the two Africans and instructed them to begin digging. The guard with the whip stood next to them so their digging was certainly energetic. Soon there was a deep hole large enough for a man to stand in.

The guards lifted the whipped man to his feet and dropped him into the hole. Only his head was above the ground level. Frantically he raised his arms and tried to hoist himself out of the hole. The bald man kicked an arm so hard Kisi thought it may have broken. The man screamed but put his arms back into the hole.

The two Africans were instructed to fill the hole. Kisi shuddered. She couldn't imagine how horrible it'd be to be buried up to her chin and unable to move. She wondered what they'd do next. Leave him in the hot sun to bake? She'd never seen or heard of anything so cruel or horrible.

Then a guard brought a clay pot to the bald-headed white boss. He went to the buried African and poured hot sugar cane syrup on the man's head. The man began screaming as the hot liquid oozed over him. The African knew, as they all did, what was next. Flies, insects, ants and mice were all attracted to the sweet syrup.

She knew this man was being used as an example to the rest of the slaves. The guards were aware this would be talked about in the slave huts for days and nights to come. Whatever this man's transgression had been, this was the price he had to pay. She wondered if the African was guilty of something or if had merely been selected for this punishment.

The red-haired and bald-headed man watched and waited. One of the guards dribbled syrup on the ground around the man to attract the insects. Soon, there was laughter among the guards as the insects began arriving. One of the guards lined up the women and pushed them toward the man buried in the ground, forcing them to stop, look and learn.

When Kisi got to the buried man, the guard held her head steady for a long look. She'd never forget what she saw. The man was shaking his head from right to left and screaming. He couldn't postpone the inevitable. His eyes were already covered with flies. A procession of black and red ants had already entered his mouth, nose and ears. She nearly fainted.

Waiting for the rest of the women and men to take their turns, she heard the man's screams becoming weaker and weaker until all she heard was a raspy whisper. Almost as if he were being choked. Then she thought of the insects eating him from the inside and again nearly fainted. How long would it take for him to die?

The red-haired man went to his white horse and stroked his head and rubbed his neck affectionately. It was obvious the horse was worth much more to him than an African slave. How could a man be so cruel to another man and yet so gentle to an animal? Kisi was filled with hate and hoped it didn't show. The two bosses finally mounted their horses and left. She knew what had just happened wasn't new to them.

She went back to her seat in the building and began, in earnest, picking seeds and leaves from the cotton like she'd never done before.

When the sun began setting, she along with the other women shuffled to their huts. They ate their evening meal quietly. When she finally laid her head on the mat she couldn't prevent the images of the man being eaten alive from coming into her mind. Finally, fitfully, she fell asleep.

The hints of a new morning pushed into her hut and Kisi arose for yet another day. Yesterday was still pressing hard into her mind but she did her best to block the intrusion.

On the way to the cotton barn, she wondered what had become of the man. Getting closer she had her answer. He was still buried in the hole but no longer alive. She wondered how long he'd endured the torture. One hour? Two? Six? Again, she shuddered as she looked at the head without eyes. The flesh was still being eaten by insects. Something much larger than ants had obviously been at work through the night.

The body stayed in the hole for two more weeks until one morning it was gone. The hole had been filled in as if nothing had ever happened.

But, Kisi saw three more holes dug only ten feet away. The holes were an ominous warning. She wondered who would be next.

Chapter 40

OVER the last three months, Atu had been watching and learning. He'd had one goal and that was to determine the best time of day to escape. Watching the guards, he'd observed a few patterns.

In the mornings, they were sharp and observant. At noon, they became more restless and less watchful. They were becoming hungry and were thinking more about food than the slaves.

Right after they'd eaten, they were alert for about an hour but then became more restless and looked like they'd really enjoy sitting by a tree and taking a nap.

In the late afternoon, they were tired and anxious to get to their homes. As dusk approached, the guards were intent on rounding up the field hands and getting out of the fields. With hundreds of Africans to deal with, there was more confusion then, than at any other time of the day.

He was convinced the best time to attempt an escape would be a few minutes before dusk. With all the slaves gathering for their walk out of the fields, would one be missed?

The dogs! He'd been watching them as well. They were always chained and each had their own master, but they were creatures of habit, just as were the guards.

He noticed the dogs were always observant for anything out of the ordinary. They'd focus on one thing and miss others. At the end of the day there would be many field hands moving about and getting into line. There would be too much movement for the dogs to focus on everyone.

His plan was coming together and his confidence was growing, but then he began wondering how he'd find the Maroons. That question would need to be answered in the mountains. Would they accept him? He still wasn't sure how soon he should make his escape. Possibly he'd watch for another month and make sure his plan had no unforeseen holes in it.

~

That evening in their hut, the men talked. One of the men said, "I had a different day today. I was part of a group working on the plantation just to the west of ours. Their plantation is next to a large river that brings water from the mountains. I had no idea there was a river there, even though it was nearly dry. It was like a river of rocks. There were huge boulders, bigger than a man, scattered through the entire river.

"Our plantation overseer apparently purchased many bundles of cotton from their plantation. Our crop wasn't large enough to fill the contract for the next ship coming in so we needed more. We spent the morning loading their cotton onto our wagons.

"The manager of the plantation there has long red hair. I remembered seeing him at the sale. I heard he's an evil man and his bald headed helper is even worse."

Then he paused, looking directly at Atu and said something that stunned him. "Atu, listen to me. While there, we were working with their Africans, some of whom were Fante. One was a woman who was carefully asking several of us if we were Fante. When I said I was, she asked if I knew a Fante named Atu. She said she was trying to find out where you were located. Her name was Darifa. She's a friend of your fiancé and was taking a risk to see if any of us knew you. I whispered to her that I knew you. She said, tell him that Kisi is on the plantation to the west of his and she's doing well. She's working in the cotton processing building next to the river."

Atu couldn't believe it. Kisi was his neighbor and she was doing well! He thanked the man again and again. His heart was racing as the men went to their mats.

He laid down but his eyes were wide open and there was no way he could get to sleep. He thought about his escape and decided he needed to get away as soon as possible.

Was it possible he could rescue Kisi and escape with her? Realistically, he knew that couldn't happen. He'd get to the mountains and then figure out his next plan.

~

Darifa couldn't wait until she'd see Kisi again and tell her what she'd learned about Atu. There wasn't much good in this new country which had become their prison, so sharing this news was exciting.

Chapter 41

THE hut was dark as pitch when Atu awoke from a restless night. The French guards hadn't unlocked the hut's wooden door yet. That would happen when the eastern sky began turning its usual pink and orange.

He knew this was his day to live or die. He couldn't believe how energized he felt as he was ready to meet his destiny. Until yesterday, he'd thought he'd wait a month before attempting his escape. But learning of Kisi's near location created an urgency that he'd not expected. It had to be today!

The door rattled and the iron clasp was removed. Their morning food was sitting on the usual bench outside the door. The men arose and their day started.

Soon they began their trek to the never-ending work. Arriving at the sugar cane fields, he was handed a machete and began his hot labor. He always worked extremely hard and fast, but today he chose to slow down. He needed to preserve some of his strength. He knew he'd need it later in the day and hoped his slow-down wouldn't be noticed.

As he swung the machete rhythmically, he ran his plan through his mind looking for what could be a life threatening mistake.

He knew those escaping in the past ran directly north through the tall sugar cane toward the mountains. He assumed the guards and dogs would expect that. Unfortunately, none of the slaves knew what types of fields lay beyond the plantation's sugar cane to the north. Possibly it was cotton or some short crop where he could be easily spotted. He couldn't take that chance. He had to use what he knew and stay away from what he didn't know.

Based on what he'd heard from the man who'd loaded cotton on the red-haired manager's plantation to the west, sugar cane ran all the way to the river. So, he'd run west through the neighboring plantation to the river.

The African's description of the river was very helpful. It was nearly dry, very wide and full of rocks, some larger than a man. That seemed like a good place to hide if needed. He also knew the river was fed by water from the mountains so if he followed the river, he'd get to where he wanted to be.

From watching in the past, he knew at the end of the work day, there would be two hundred field hands gathered next to the cane field waiting for the walk to their huts. He assumed ultimately there would be too many scents for the dogs to sort through in trying to find his. He smiled as he thought about what was to happen very soon.

He still didn't have a plan on how to meet the Maroons, or how he could rescue Kisi. He knew the Maroons were skilled in keeping their freedom and he was anxious to join them. But, he still had a hard day before attempting an escape.

~

The day was long and hot but he continued his cutting as the sun continued its journey to the western horizon. Glancing up, he estimated he was about thirty minutes from 'run-time'.

He was glad he was going alone though he'd have enjoyed the companionship of another man or two. But keeping his plans quiet was the safest. He knew there were Africans who wouldn't hesitate snitching on another slave for a returned favor or two. Maintaining secrecy reduced the likelihood that the guards would do retaliation against those remaining. The less anyone knew the better.

The sun was nearing the horizon. The slaves were coming in from the fields to the clearing. He joined a group as they walked toward the growing crowd of Africans. He knew there'd be about ten or twelve guards and six dogs managing this large group. The line started forming. Edging slowly backward to the end of the line, he was only ten feet from the cane field.

Suddenly a dog barked, then they all started barking. Looking forward he saw a man on the ground. Atu assumed the man had merely stumbled and fell but he was still receiving multiple lashes. He knew the dogs were alert, but he also knew they were focused on the fallen man, as were the guards. There wouldn't be a better time, so he slipped backwards into the cane.

The cane was thick. The stalks were tall. He was barely inside the field, so he carefully moved deeper into the cane. He hoped no African would sound an alarm! There was no more barking and he could hear the men shuffling away. He waited. Could it be this easy? His heart was racing and fear was gripping his throat. He knew if he was caught now, he'd be brutally beaten and likely killed.

He was tempted to run, but he knew the noise the cane stalks would make if he barged through the forest of cane. His work in cutting cane had always been on the perimeter. He couldn't believe how dense the field was... but he still had the machete!

Though his racing heart told him to run, he knew what he needed to do. He waited. No dogs. No guards. He waited some more. Dusk was his friend. He couldn't believe how quiet it was. There was no barking, yelling or clanking shackles. Everything was deathly quiet...

Almost a year earlier he'd been squatting among the ferns in Guinea waiting for a bongo antelope. He'd surprised his Fante tribesmen by killing the bongo and had been regarded as a young successful hunter. He felt those same African survival skills surging within him now. They were centuries old and genetically he knew those instincts for hunting and survival were strong. He knew they'd serve him well over the next few days.

He began quietly moving west. Continually west toward the river. He resisted the temptation of going north to the mountains. It would be shorter but there were simply too many unknowns. So he continued, knowing when he got to the river, he could follow it to the mountains.

There would be no running through the cane. It was too dense. He continued pushing his way through the field making as little noise as possible.

Suddenly he broke into an open area and realized it was a dirt lane wide enough for a sugar cane cart. Taking the lane to the left would lead to the plantations and the right would take him to the mountains. In the dim moonlight ahead, he could see the neighboring plantation's cane field which he knew went to the river.

He decided quickly to follow the path to the right since it was running north to the mountains. Since there were cane fields on both sides of the lane, he could always jump into the cane and get to the river if necessary.

Now, he could run and he did. A long, loping run that he knew he could do for miles. The mountains were still another five or six miles north but he didn't know how far the path went. The freedom and air in his face was beyond anything he could have imagined!

Three miles or so later, the lane ended. He stopped and listened. Nothing but quiet. Ahead of him was a large cotton field. To his left was more cane. Looking all around, he couldn't see any lights. Listening carefully, there was only quiet. Could it be that simple?

He began running north through the cotton. The rows ran toward the mountains so his flight was easy. He hadn't been this free for a long time. In the moonlight, he couldn't see the mountains before him, but he knew he was getting closer.

Suddenly there was a loud crashing noise off to his left. Crouching down, the moonlight allowed him a glimpse of three deer he'd startled.

Continuing to run, he felt as free as the deer. Then the cotton field abruptly ended. He leaned over, examined a bush and found it to be coffee. He knew it was grown in the foothills or on mountains so he knew he was getting closer to his destination.

Again, he ran for five minutes in the coffee plant rows until they ended in vegetation. Stopping again, he saw trees, ferns and undergrowth. He looked for lights. None. He listened for dogs. Quiet. There was a slight breeze and the usual night sounds. He hadn't had to use the river to get to the mountains, but he now knew the lay of this foreign land he was in.

He continued into the forest and knew he was going uphill. His heart was racing, not from exertion, but anticipation of what was ahead. There was fear, but it was different. This fear was no longer about the French white men, but whether he'd be accepted among the Maroons if and when he'd find them. Would they think he was a spy sent by the French? Would any of them know his Fante language?

He climbed higher and higher. There were no paths, but this was so much like his Africa, he felt at home. He wondered if this land had bongo antelopes. Or hyenas? Or wild dogs or lions? He'd not thought about that before and decided to put his instincts to work.

Finally, he stopped under a large mahogany tree. He began climbing and found a spot where he could nestle securely into two large limbs. Settling in, he instantly was reminded of another tree, another time – a time of watching elephants in the Kakum River in Guinea with Kisi.

Looking out over the plains, he saw no lights. Listening, he heard no dogs. He fell asleep, free!

~

He opened his eyes and for a moment thought he was in his hut. The sky above him was just beginning to turn pink. He quickly descended from his perch and continued north. He didn't know how far the guards would travel into the mountains before giving up, fearful of the Maroons.

The tropical forest was a lot like his African home. There was plenty of water and trees with nuts and fruit. He plodded deeper and deeper, away from the plantation, hard labor, certain death... and Kisi.

Now on his third day away from the plantation, he saw something on the ground which stopped him cold, in his tracks. On the ground ahead of him was the rind and pit from a mango! Someone had been here recently. He looked for a trail and found it. His hunting in Africa had been all about tracking and it was now put to good use.

He knew from the small and light indent in the soil that the person was likely a woman. The person had been alone and was moving to the east. He carefully and quietly followed the trail.

Then, he heard a hacking noise like a machete cutting cane. He quietly moved toward the sound. It was getting louder. He was getting closer. Then he saw the source. An African man was cutting down a small tree with a machete. Watching him was a woman and a small child. There was a hut behind them which was obviously their home.

Atu cautiously stepped out of the brush. The child saw him and said something to the man, who quickly paused his machete in mid-air and stared at him.

The man said something which Atu didn't understand. Atu slowly moved toward him. The man was talking and smiling.

Here in the mountains, another African wasn't a threat. The two men grasped one another's hand and smiled broadly.

The African motioned Atu to meet his family. The woman was pleasant and offered him dried meat and plantains. He sat, ate and watched as the man finished cutting down the tree. Then Atu stood, picked up another machete and began trimming the branches from the tree. It felt like he was once again in Africa. It felt like home.

The African man began chanting a strange language as they rhythmically swung their machetes together. It was a different language, but the methodical beat was the same as Fante and the guttural clicks the man was making seemed familiar.

Finished, the man motioned for Atu to follow him. Quickly disappearing into the thick and green undergrowth, Atu followed.

Their path eventually opened into a clearing. Atu was surprised to see another group of people. Four families. Men, women and a few children. They looked up but weren't alarmed to see a strange African approaching.

He said 'Hello' in Fante. A man quickly stepped forward and returned his greeting. They embraced. Animatedly, they began talking.

The man said, "My name is Yooku. I am Fante from Guinea in Africa."

"Ah, my name is Atu and I am Fante from Guinea in Africa."

They smiled.

"Look around you Atu. There are many Africans in the mountains who've escaped the white men. When the French venture into the mountains, we kill them. Some we maim and send back to their plantations as a message. They usually leave us alone." Then he smiled and continued, "But we don't leave them alone."

"How many Africans are here?"

"There are many here in the mountains, to the east and the west. We're about 200 here in this area. There are over 125 men, the rest being women and children. Some of the Maroons have been in the mountains for many years. I found my way here over five years ago. My wife and I have two children."

Hesitating, Atu asked, "Yooku, how may I join your village?"

"Atu, you're already in our village. You're already a part of our family. An old Fante proverb says, *'If it's not good for everyone, it's good for no one.'* This good place belongs to you, me and to all free Africans."

Atu laughed and said, "I know that proverb. It reminds me of another which my father told me, *'Two ants together can pull one grasshopper.'*

Smiling, Yooku said, "Come. I want you to meet others."

Disappearing into the jungle, Atu followed. Soon they emerged into a clearing much larger than that of Yooku's. There were many more people.

The afternoon was filled with Yooku introducing Atu to many other families in the mountains. Some were Fante, most were not, but they were all Africans.

They returned to Yooku's clearing and he said, "Let's get started making a home for you. Tomorrow we have a special gathering."

~

The next afternoon, Yooku and his family, Atu and the others headed to the much larger clearing to the north where they'd been the day before.

When they arrived, Atu was amazed at how many Africans were already gathered, and more were coming. He smelled cooking meat and his mouth watered. Above a charcoal fire, he saw a pig being roasted. Women were busy at other fires. Children were running and playing. His eyes filled with tears as he remembered his Fante village, mother, father and friends in Africa.

Then someone thrust a wooden cup into his hand. He sipped it. It was very sweet and made from fruit. He'd not had anything like it before.

Yooku said, "You can thank the French for this drink. The juice is ground up mango, but we've added sugar from the cane plantation below. We gladly use their products for our benefit. We don't want to forget that this sugar was made by our African cousins on the plain of Les Cayes."

"How do you get the sugar?"

"Oh, you'll see soon enough, my friend. Tomorrow night we'll show you!"

~

The afternoon went by quickly and soon it was dusk. A fire was burning in the middle of the clearing and was surrounded by approximately seventy people.

Yooku said, "You'll be asked to speak of your life in Africa and here at the plantation. Everyone is always anxious to hear news of what's happening outside the mountains. Many have been here long enough to have learned Fante and other dialects, but if someone doesn't understand you, someone else will tell them."

Yooku stood and invited Atu to stand with him. Soon, the crowd grew quiet.

Yooku said, "Atu, tell your new family about your village in Africa and your story before arriving here in our mountains."

Atu began and soon the story of the capture of he and Kisi, their journey on the ship and arrival in Hispaniola spilled out to waiting ears. He knew his story wasn't much different than the listeners, but they were leaning forward waiting to hear more.

Someone asked, "Where is Kisi now?"

He said, "She's working on the plain, next to the river of rocks. She's working in the cotton building."

Atu heard several grunts from the men and Yooku said, "They know the plantation and the place she works."

After the village feast and meeting was over, a man came to Atu and simply said, "We'll find Kisi for you and bring her here."

Atu looked at him in shock. "How can you do that?"

"Didn't you know that some of us have been here for many years? Our women didn't find their own way to us. As men, we knew how to escape and survive. Without women, our tribe would soon die. I think destiny has brought you to us. We'll find Kisi for you. We know how to do that."

He disappeared into the darkness. Soon Yooku, his family and the rest moved into the darkness to their clearing.

That night, under the stars, Atu stared into the sky. He smiled. He was again filled with hope.

~

The next day was Atu's tenth day in the mountains. He had now finished his single room, dirt-floor, thatched hut. Standing inside, he looked around with pride. He'd started building, but then had decided to double it in size. He was now hopeful of starting a family.

Yooku came to him at noon and said, "This afternoon we'll leave for the plains on a raiding party. There's a plantation we need to visit. You can join us and learn."

Midafternoon, men gathered in the large clearing. Most had machetes but there were clubs, spears, bows and arrows as well.

Ten men, including Atu began walking single file through the jungle heading west and then south. They began their trek down the mountain side before dusk. Two hours after dark, they were in the fields of the plain and still heading south. Far into the distance, Atu saw flickering lights. They continued and Atu realized this wasn't a new journey for these men.

The lights were becoming brighter, and yet the men continued moving forward through a cotton field. Atu listened and all was quiet. Even after many years, these men had not forgotten their African ways! Atu felt a shiver roll over him as he once again was in the planation fields. Memories of hard labor, whips and dogs rushed into his mind. But at the same time, he felt the strength and confidence of the men surrounding him and moved forward.

The lights they'd seen were torches set on poles surrounding a distant plantation house. A large storage barn loomed a few hundred feet to the right. The group carefully moved toward it. One of the men quietly moved to the back of the barn, knelt in the dirt and began loosening a board. Soon, it was lying on the ground and just as quickly, another. The man paused, listened and scooted under the board and into the barn. Then another three men did the same.

Within two minutes, boxes and sacks were pushed out of the opening. Then more. Quickly, the four men emerged. The boards were reattached.

One of the men used a cotton plant to smooth the ground at the back of the building, wiping away traces of their trespass. Each man hoisted a box or sack and began their retreat north to the mountains.

There'd been no dogs and no alarms. Likely there was enough in the barn that what little they took wouldn't even be missed. All was quiet. Atu's heart swelled with pride at the skills of his African brothers.

He smelled meat in the sack he was carrying on his back. He also carried a large bag of rice in his arms. The Maroon had been correct when he'd said, *"The white men leave us alone, but we don't leave them alone."*

They arrived in their clearing before dawn and Atu wearily laid down on his mat in his new hut. He'd been surprised at how efficiently the Maroon's had been able to pilfer the plantation's goods. If they could do that, then possibly rescuing Kisi was a possibility, but no doubt it would be more difficult. He happily fell asleep.

Chapter 42

February 10, 1778 – Labreche Plantation – Les Cayes, Saint-Domingue

KISI expertly picked the leaves, twigs and seeds from yet another boll of cotton. It'd been another long day in a string of endless days. It'd soon be a year that she and Atu had been abducted and there was never a day she didn't think about him. In fact, he was about all she'd thought about.

Unknown to her, there were two African Maroons crouching in the sugar cane field adjacent to the Labreche plantation's cotton processing building. The Maroon mountain group had decided to fulfill their promise to Atu in an attempt to rescue Kisi.

Yooku and Atu remained motionless. Then they crept to the edge of the field and peered through the stalks. Atu's heart nearly stopped when he saw Kisi working with the other women. He pointed her out to Yooku and whispered a single word, "Kisi."

They retreated further into the cane to join five other Maroons. They quietly waited. Attempting a rescue during daylight had been a dangerous decision, but it was the only way to have Kisi in a position of potentially being saved. No one was minimizing the danger as they all felt the tension in the air. Atu saw fear on the faces of the Maroons but he was also strengthened by their assurance and smiles.

The sun was setting in the west and soon, the guards would begin calling the slaves in from the cotton and cane fields. It seemed that time had stopped but soon they heard the first commands of the guards.

The field-hands began gathering in the clearing outside the cotton building. As the crowd of slaves grew larger, Yooku cautiously emerged from the cane and moved into the crowd.

The mass of men and women started shuffling the mile to their huts toward the south. Sugar cane was growing on the right and left.

Kisi automatically followed the group as she had countless other days, surrounded by her fellow African slaves.

Then, like a shadow, a man was beside her and whispered, "Kisi."

Startled, she looked into the eyes of a man she'd not seen before who told her in Fante, "Be still. Look forward and walk with me. I'll take you to Atu."

Her black eyes flashed as she heard Atu's name. Could this be happening?

Yooku casually moved to the middle of the two hundred field hands and then moved closer to the right hand edge. Kisi followed. Ahead was a curving bend in the lane. Yooku said, "When we make the turn ahead, we'll quickly and quietly go into the cane on the right. The guards ahead can't see this far back and the guards at the back can't see around the bend. We'll do it when I see the middle guards looking forward."

The bend was approaching and Kisi's heart was beating wildly. She still had an image in her mind of the African being eaten alive by insects and knew what would happen if they were caught. She also knew she needed to trust this unknown man if she ever wanted to see Atu again.

Then, the bend was twenty paces away. Then ten. Then five. The guard was looking ahead and Yooku grabbed Kisi's wrist and pulled her into the cane. Almost immediately, he forced her to the ground. The slaves shuffled past. Would a slave sound an alarm?

The guard on his horse with two dogs was bringing up the rear. Yooku and Kisi held their breaths and remained motionless though they were only six feet into the field. The guard, his horse and dogs were coming closer. Closer. Then they were past. They waited.

Two minutes later, Yooku began moving north in the cane. It was tough walking and there was no time for talk. Kisi followed obediently through the tall stalks. Then suddenly, there were six Africans crouching quietly in a small cleared patch of cane. One of them was Atu!

She ran into his arms and wept. Yooku hurriedly said, "Quickly now. We must go. The dogs will be coming."

Kisi knew exactly what was happening back at the slave village. About now the group would be arriving and there would be a count of men and women. When the guard would find her missing, he'd take the dogs to her mat to catch her scent. Then the hunt would be on.

Fifteen minutes later, the Maroons stopped their tedious journey through the sugarcane. Then the men did something unexpected. They began clearing the cane around them with machetes. Soon, they had an opening in the middle of the cane field that was about twenty-five feet in diameter. They quickly stacked the cut cane in a pile in the center of the clearing. Six of the Maroons spaced themselves around the pile facing outward. Atu helped Kisi climb up onto the stack of cut cane and then took a spot in the circle of Maroons. The Maroons stood quietly with their machetes and clubs ready for battle. Each intently listened for the dogs and stared at the tall wall of standing cane before them.

In the distance they began hearing the barking of dogs which were apparently now hot on Kisi's trail. One of the men said, "I think there are four."

The barking became louder. Louder. They could hear the crashing of the sugar cane as the hounds made their way toward them. The dogs sensed the Africans were close. Suddenly with a fierce snarling growl the first dog tore through the tall cane perimeter and was stopped instantly by a machete. Three more behind the first met their fate just as quickly.

Yooku said, "There'll be no more dogs. It's too dense for the horses and the white men won't risk coming in on foot. We're free to go."

They continued working their way through the cane and emerged onto a lane heading north toward the mountains. Atu and Kisi were in the center of the small group holding hands and smiling.

Kisi was still in shock. There had been no advance notice about the rescue. There had been no time to hope or even think about the future. Suddenly Atu was here. They were safe. They were free.

Atu smiled and said, "Kisi, almost a year ago we were walking into our jungle when we were first engaged. Do you remember that I wanted to show you something special?"

"Yes, I remember. You wanted to show me the mineral waters at the river where the elephants gathered."

"Yes. That was the best and happiest day of my life, being with you. That day was also my worst. We had a beautiful time together but I failed to protect you from the slave traders. I've felt nothing but shame since then. After I killed the bongo, I thought of myself in a proud way. I was puffed up. I was the great hunter, respected by all in the village. Then I became the man who received the most beautiful bride in the village. There wasn't anything better. I should've been more careful."

He continued, "Now here we are again. Walking into a jungle."

Stopping in the lane, he looked into her moonlit eyes and said, "Over the last year I've been repeating the same words over and over again. They've helped me get through all the tough times. I think you'd like to know my words...

"I am Atu. I am a Fante warrior and tribesman. I've killed a bongo antelope with my own spear. I am a respected man of my village. A woman of great beauty has been chosen to be my wife. I've now survived some of the most horrible things put on a man. I will survive. I will live."

He smiled and said, "Kisi, you're my betrothed and I have something special I want to show you in the mountains."

Tears filled her eyes as they embraced.

They ran together, hands clasped, to catch the small band of Maroons now ahead of them. Their future lay before them, far removed from the horror and tragedy of the plains.

Chapter 43

May 10, 1793 – Mountains North of Les Cayes, Saint-Domingue

KISI was picking berries for her family. Her fingers expertly picked the ripe ones and left those still not quite ready. Her memories floated back fifteen years to the time she'd picked seeds, twigs and leaves from the plantation's cotton bolls. Living peacefully as Maroons in the mountains had caused time to pass quickly. Kneeling next to the large bush, she decided she had enough for the next week.

Standing, she looked out over the plains to the south and thought about her past. Though unable to see the Labreche plantation or the countless black Africans working in the many fields, the memories hadn't escaped her. She'd never be able to repay Yooku or the other Africans who put their lives in jeopardy many years ago, to rescue her from what had been certain death. Everything that had happened since then had been a sweet gift.

Suddenly, she heard a scream which brought her back to reality. Running quickly with her basket of berries she emerged into a nearby mountain clearing.

Her youngest daughter, six-year-old Morowa was sitting on a limb of a large mango tree about eight feet off the ground. Her eyes were filled with fear. Standing below her was her older brother Kobi. At ten-years-old, he enjoyed tormenting his younger sister.

Morowa screamed again and said, "Mama! He convinced me to climb the tree, but now I'm afraid to get down. Kobi said he wouldn't help me and that I'd need to live in the tree. He said I'm now a monkey."

"Kobi, that's no way to treat your little sister. Help her."

With a broad smile he'd inherited from his father Atu, he held his arms up and said, "Jump!"

"No, you won't catch me!"

"Yes I will. Trust me."

Leaning forward she fell into his arms. Hugging her he said, "See, I told you I'd catch you."

Kisi began walking and told her two children to follow her. She was incredibly proud of her family and her constant contented smile proved that fact to everyone who knew her.

Emerging from the jungle into another large clearing, they walked past twelve huts before getting to their own. The village the Maroons had built was almost like her Fante village in Africa. This was home.

Kisi saw Abena, her oldest child, sitting on a mat outside their home, preparing a soup for their noon meal. She was so pleased with her fourteen-year-old daughter and the example she set for the rest of her children. Abena never complained and was always willing to help. She couldn't believe Abena was almost the same age she herself had been when abducted in Guinea. She also couldn't escape the fact that Abena was nearly the same age she'd been when betrothed to Atu.

She knelt to help Abena with the soup while Morowa took the berries into the hut to prepare them for the meal. Hearing voices, she turned toward the jungle and saw Atu with their twelve-year-old son Agyei.

Though Kobi had the quick smile and humor of his father, Agyei had his hunting skills. Both Atu and Agyei were holding rabbits from a successful hunting trip in the lowland hills in the north. The men of their mountain village had learned to go north for their hunting rather than to the plains to the south. They all knew the dangers of the southern plains and had no desire to relive those memories.

Of course, the plains had to be visited periodically for practical reasons. The village needed items such as cotton, tobacco, sugar and rice. Night-time raids to the plantations were usually successful. Since she'd arrived in the mountains fifteen years earlier, they'd lost several men on raids, but normally the men returned safely with plenty of bounty they could use.

Another reason they raided the plantations was more strategic and personal. Revenge and havoc. The raids created chaos among the French. Over the years it was obvious the French feared the Maroons in the nearby mountains. Never in fifteen years had the white men ventured anywhere close to their mountain village. They had always turned back in the much lower foothills. The raiding Maroons had become adept in using the river and the cane fields as their escape routes.

Atu and Agyei walked to the hut and dropped five rabbits on the ground. Atu yelled, "Kobi, I need you."

Kobi broke away from three other boys he'd been playing with and joined his father. When he spied the rabbits, he went into their hut and emerged with a knife and large wooden bowl. Picking up the rabbits, he disappeared behind the hut into the jungle.

Atu smiled at Kisi. "You've done a fine job in teaching our children how to be Fante."

"It's in their blood, but we've done well, haven't we?"

Atu smiled again as he thought about his life. He only wished their parents could be around to enjoy their grandchildren. It still angered him that slavery had ripped the two of them from their African home. It had also hurt their village and family in Africa. Their raiding trips to the plantations weren't enough to diminish his anger and thirst for revenge. He wasn't alone in his feelings.

Here in the mountains there were many villages of Maroons. The slaves had come from various places in Africa, each with their own language. Many had learned the white man's language of French. Over time, a new dialect developed among the Maroons which incorporated words from their African dialects as well as the French language. They now had the ability to communicate in a common tongue.

After eating their noon meal, Atu and Kisi walked into the jungle. As they walked on the familiar path, Atu said, "On our hunting trip, I heard some news. We talked to men from a Maroon village in the east. It seems some rebellions by Maroons are starting to happen.

"The men told us about a revolt which took place over a year ago many miles to the northeast. An escaped slave named Boukman, along with 100,000 slaves led an uprising against the French. Thousands of French were killed and hundreds of coffee and cane plantations were destroyed. The French then attacked the slaves and thousands of Africans were killed. The men told us to continue our raids on the plantations here in Les Cayes. More revolts are going to happen."

Kisi replied, "Our life here in the mountains is peaceful. We're able to have families and live almost like we did in Africa. I'm worried about more revolts. It might be like poking a stick into a hornets nest."

"That's true, I'm sure. But if Yooku had chosen to live safely and comfortably in the mountains, you wouldn't have been rescued."

Then Atu stopped and said, "I'm sorry Kisi, I was only saying there are many slaves on the plains who would like to join us in the mountains. Tonight the men will have a meeting to decide what we will do."

Atu knew exactly what Kisi was feeling and he felt torn. But he himself had been given a gift when Yooku thought beyond himself. Without him stepping forward, Kisi wouldn't be here with him and their four children wouldn't have been born.

He continued, "An old proverb says that the two most important gifts to give a child are roots and wings. We need to keep telling them about Africa so they know where they came from. At the same time we need to tell them how beautiful freedom is."

~

That evening there were forty men gathered around the village clearing. Atu shared what he'd heard from the men in the northeast.

Atu knew these men around the fire very well and knew there'd be many different opinions.

He said, "The men encouraged us to continue our raids on the plantations on the plains. They said there were many mountain villages of Maroons from the north to the south in the country and rebellions would be growing. The Maroon villages should wait to hear the drumbeats and pass them on. It won't take long for all the Marron villages to hear the drums. He said when we hear them it will be time to begin the revolt."

A man near Atu quickly said, "We live a peaceful life here. It seems we're begging for trouble by rising against the French."

Another man said, "I agree. The French are leaving us alone and even tolerating our raids. They're afraid of us. What if we join the revolt and fail? How many of us will die?"

An older man at the front of the group said, "I was born free in Africa and have been here in Hispaniola for thirty-four years. I don't have much longer to live, but you young men have many years ahead of you. You're free here in the mountains, but it's not true freedom because there are those in the plains who want to enslave you. I can't fight, but if I were a young man, I'd use my machete for more than cutting brush!"

A young man interjected, "I have many friends on the plantations below and their lives are slipping away. They're slaves knowing only hardship and death. We who are free-men owe those men and women on the plains something. We need to give them a chance. They can't experience freedom without us making it possible."

The conversation continued into the night, but in the end an old African summed it up and established the future direction. "I've listened all night to your many opinions and thoughts. Some of us ran away from slavery many years ago. Some of you are newly free. Some were slaves for many years and for some here, you were only slaves for a year. Some were born in Africa and that's still fresh in your minds.

Others of you were born on the plantation to parents and grandparents who only knew slavery. We're all different. But, one thing is certain. Every man deserves to be free. We should do what we can to bring freedom to our African brothers and sisters."

The old man continued, "I think history will speak kindly of us if we rebel against the horrors and tragedy of this slavery. What do you say? Shall we do our part to end this?"

The men around the fire enthusiastically uttered their support for what had been said.

Yooku said, "I'm getting older. Taking the lead with what's ahead is beyond my years. I'd suggest Atu should begin our planning for the future. There's a lot to be done in preparation for the sound of the drums. To overcome the slavery, we must join hands with the other Maroon villages here in the south."

The group was eager to support the leadership of Atu.

Atu said, "I'm willing, but I'll need many men to walk beside me."

The men gave their support for Atu and the meeting was over.

Chapter 44

July 18, 1793 – Labreche Plantation in Les Cayes, Saint-Domingue

SYLVAIN and Jeanne were sitting at dusk in their courtyard talking about their day. She'd just received a letter from their oldest daughter Inez, who was living in Paris. A French ship bringing more Africans to the docks had just brought the correspondence to the island.

She was reading the letter to Sylvain. *"Our family is well. Elizabeth is now three-years-old and growing. She's been talking for quite some time and is getting into everything. Mother, she has eyes like yours and Father's laugh. I can't believe I've been gone from Les Cayes for seven years already. Louise and I still spend a lot of time together and she seems to be getting along well with Alfred. We all were happy that you could be here for her wedding two years ago. Louise and I were talking recently and we think it would be good to bring our families to Les Cayes for a visit. Possibly early next year we can make the trip. How are things going at the..."*

Abruptly, Sylvain interrupted, "There they go again. What do you think the meaning of those drums might be? I heard them all day yesterday and now again. I'd guess it's the Maroons in the mountains harassing us again. The overseers told me that the drums are making our slaves restless."

"I'm worried Sylvain. There were huge uprisings north of the capital the last two years. Now there's rumors the English and Spanish are supporting the free-blacks and Maroons in an overthrow of the French in Saint-Domingue. Since France declared war on Britain this year, it seems like everything's in a turmoil. We've had a wonderful and peaceful time here and I hope that doesn't change."

Sylvain, deep in thought, said, "Francois and I have worked hard in maintaining discipline of our Africans. They know better than to try to do something foolish. There'd be a huge price for them to pay. Anyway, I think it's time to put those thoughts away and go to bed."

~

A shrill scream in his yard woke Sylvain shortly after midnight. Dressing quickly he went to his front porch and immediately saw flames rising from one of his plantation barns a half mile away. He ran inside and pulled his flintlock musket and pistol from the wall. Picking up his sword, he buckled it to his belt and ran out the front door. He yelled to Jeanne, "There's a fire. I'll see what's going on! Stay inside."

Running toward the barn, he was joined by his overseers and many guards. Arriving out of breath, he knew the barn was full of hay and straw for the plantation's horses and mules. It was obvious they'd be losing the barn, as it was burning with a vengeance. Flames were leaping high into the air and the sounds of horses and mules in the barn were horrendous. The fire was so intense, no one was even trying to rescue the horses.

Sylvain asked one of the overseers, "Has anyone been able to get any of the horses or mules out?"

"No, by the time we arrived, it was too hot for anyone to go in."

Sylvain stood by helplessly, along with many of his men whose faces were illuminated by the flames and tragedy unfolding in front of them. Without these horses and mules, the slaves would be working much harder until more horses could be purchased. Already, he was starting to see the profit margins of the plantation taking a huge hit.

He asked one of the overseers, "Does anyone have any idea how the fire started?"

"No. No one heard or saw anything, but it was likely started by Maroon raiders!"

The fire continued burning and then Sylvain heard a distant scream. Turning around, he saw flames erupting from Francois' home.

With terror gripping his chest, he began running. Now, more men began following him.

Arriving out of breath a few minutes later, they saw there was nothing to do but watch as the home burned. He yelled for Francois and Marie but heard only the fire which was quickly devouring their home. Walking around the home, he saw something lying on the ground.

Side by side in the grass were three bloody bodies. Francois and Marie had been brutally killed by machete and dragged out of the house. The third body was his own wife Jeanne. The scene before him was horrible. He uttered a low groan that increased in volume until it erupted into an agonizing scream.

Turning around he saw flames engulfing his own home as well as the large Labreche family mansion.

Suddenly, he began seeing black shapes emerging from the shadows of the flame-lit buildings of the plantation. One of the overseers yelled, "Maroons! Maroons!"

Sylvain took aim at one of the black men running toward him. The flash from the powder and thunder from the gun erupted and filled the night. The African crumbled to the ground only six feet from Sylvain, his machete still held tightly in his clenched hand. Then more guns thundered. Sylvain used his pistol to stop yet another African and then he pulled his sword.

In the end, their swords weren't enough and the guns took too long to reload. There were simply too many Maroons and too few French.

By dawn, the plantation's buildings were smoldering ruins. There were French and African bodies scattered in the plantation's courtyards. Some of the French guards and overseers had tried to escape into the fields, but to no avail. It'd been a massacre.

The mountain Maroons had their night of vengeance in Les Cayes.

A half mile behind the destroyed plantation homes were the African huts. The slaves heard the gunfire throughout the night as well as the ensuing commotion. The twelve guards watching the slave village were apprehensive and waited.

Then, running out of the fields surrounding the village, the Maroons attacked the guards and ruthlessly killed them. The slaves heard the victory cries of the Maroons. Cowering in their huts, they waited. Soon, the Maroons began tearing off the locks and doors of the huts. The enslaved Africans quietly emerged. Their ingrained submission and years of captivity prevented them from comprehending what had just happened.

Ultimately, they had to be convinced that they were free to leave the compound. They followed their rescuers north through the fields toward the mountains, toward freedom.

Atu and his son Agyei stood in the yard of the burnt out homes. The yard was strewn with bodies. Some of the white bodies were now headless. Those heads were now perched on top of tall wooden stakes. They were a testimony of the anger, hatred and years of torment the Africans had endured.

Looking around, he saw a head with flowing red hair spiked on the top of a stake. Nearby was the bald head of Sylvain on yet another. Vengeance had been dealt. The heads would serve as an indication of the lengths to which the Africans would go to secure freedom.

Atu turned his back on the plantation and followed the thousand freed slaves to the mountains.

~

That night, the Maroons had destroyed anything related to the French. The Labreche and Boudet plantations had been utterly demolished, as had many others in the plains. There were no white men, women or children left alive. Once started, the revolt took hold with a vengeance. The pent up anger which had been stifled for years exploded into a rage that knew no bounds. It had been like a wildfire being blown by a strong wind through dry timber and brush.

As Atu began his ascent up the mountain path to his village with the newly freed slaves, he stopped with Agyei and looked south. They saw the smoke coming from the smoldering ruins of the Labreche and Boudet plantations. Looking east toward the rising sun, they saw many other pillars of smoke rising into the morning sky.

He said, "Agyei, this was a night no one will forget. It's the beginning of the end for the French and the beginning of the future for the African. I'm thankful we could share this night together."

He continued, "There was a time sixteen years ago when I killed a bongo antelope and returned to my village as a man. I think tonight, you'll return to our village as a man."

Putting his arm around his son, they walked home together.

Chapter 45

September 12, 1810 – Aboard *The Diligent* on the North Atlantic

MIA stood along the gunwale looking at the dark blue Atlantic. Her eyes caught a movement off the starboard side and she watched as dolphins followed the English ship.

She couldn't believe she was on her first voyage. Her mind began wandering through the past years of her life.

Born in 1764 in Paris, she'd led a sheltered life. Her parents had been wealthy and spared nothing in getting their children the best education. She'd graduated from the Universite de Paris in 1787 with a degree in Philosophy.

In 1789, her life took an unexpected turn. She met a young man in a Paris café. When their eyes met, something happened. It was the beginning of a courtship.

He was a man of the world yet driven by principles, morality and values. Her philosophy background and his principles made for some interesting dialogues. Her family had accepted him quickly and their marriage a year later had been blessed.

The couple had been disappointed in their inability to conceive children. However, her career as a Parisian private school tutor and teacher blossomed quickly and she loved her work of nurturing and filling young minds.

Her husband had been on a different path. Due to adverse experiences in his youth he had become disenchanted with the wealth, rituals and aristocracy of the French Catholic Church and decided to attend a Protestant theological seminary in French-speaking Lausanne, Switzerland.

Returning to Paris in 1787 after five years at Lausanne, he had difficulty in finding a Protestant church to pastor, so he decided to start his own. It had a slow beginning since Catholicism was the official

religion of France. Then in 1789 the French Revolution began. The Catholic churches in France floundered over the next ten years and were nearly obliterated. He worked diligently and quietly with his small Protestant congregation for twenty years, but was frustrated in not making a larger difference in the world. Then, in 1804, news from the New World changed his life and of course, her own.

Her thoughts were interrupted by a voice behind her. "Mia! Did you see the dolphins?"

"Yes Pierre, I've been watching them."

Then, noticing a sad look in his eyes she asked, "What's troubling you?"

Pierre, hesitating, responded, "Oh, I was below deck. You can't imagine the memories I'm having by being aboard a ship in the middle of the Atlantic again. They're not all good memories."

Looking at the horizon, he continued, "I spent countless hours with Captain Jean on a ship such as this on our six month voyage. He had told me to visit him in his old age in Paris, but that didn't happen. Pirates boarded his ship on a voyage to Saint-Domingue and he was killed in 1782. This trip is bringing back many memories."

Over their twenty years together, Pierre had shared literally everything he'd experienced and felt on his voyage to Hispaniola in 1777. She knew this current voyage, thirty-three years later, would reopen his old wounds. He'd lived with ongoing nightmares throughout their marriage as she'd watched helplessly.

News of the destruction of the various Saint-Domingue French plantations had reached France quickly in 1793. Pierre felt compelled to gather as much information as he could about what was happening, specifically in the southwest of Hispaniola.

Uprisings in Les Cayes by the Maroons in 1793 had only been the beginning of revolts taking place over the next ten years. Then in 1804, a successful rebellion by the 500,000 slaves against the 35,000 French had ended slavery in Saint-Domingue. Now, the ex-slaves had their own country which they called Haiti. France and other nations had given up seeking to re-establish control over the Pearl of the Antilles, but Pierre knew the Africans would have great difficulty in succeeding as a country. The African's lack of education and years of being dominated would take its toll.

He believed without the pure Gospel message of Jesus Christ, success would be minimal for the Africans. He felt profoundly called to bring the Gospel, but he wanted it to be different than how the Spanish, English and French had brought it before.

From 1492 to 1804, the Gospel in Saint-Domingue had been intricately intertwined with impure motives, the pursuits of business, profits and gold. He believed deeply the Gospel had to be only about the shed blood, death, burial and resurrection of Jesus Christ. That, in itself, would change lives and help to provide the principles and values for the new country.

"Mia, are you afraid?"

Hesitantly she replied, "Yes. But your passion and vision give me a strength I don't naturally have. I trust God and I trust you. I know beyond a doubt He's called you to this work."

His face tensed, "When I think back to my voyage to Les Cayes thirty-three years ago, I can still picture the African's faces. I can see their fear and terror. I can almost smell the stench of that first trip. I still have the sound of their screams in my head. I had my own fears then, but they were nothing compared to what the Africans endured.

"The horrors and tragedies the Africans experienced over the last three hundred years have changed them forever. Unfortunately, they were exposed to a distorted type of Christianity that's very different from the pure Gospel. I'm getting older but I want to try to fix that, if they'll listen and if I live long enough. Their anger, fear and desire for revenge might prevent that from happening. But, I can't begin to tell you how excited I am to step foot on the Les Cayes dock once again. One thing I know, it'll be very different than the first time. The Haitians would never permit a French ship to land there, but they'll welcome *The Diligent* since its carrying the English flag."

Pierre wrapped his arm around Mia. Looking forward over the bowsprit, he knew it was pointing them to their new home.

He said, "The last time I was here, we took everything from the Africans, including their lives and hope. This time Mia, we're here to give our lives, and to give the Haitians an opportunity for eternal life. This time it'll be different!"

Their trunks, stowed below in the hold, had what they needed to live their lives to the very end in this new country called Haiti. Five additional trunks were filled with French Bibles and hope.

With a faraway look, he said, "Wouldn't it be a miracle if we could meet an African who had been on the *L'ange D'or* with me?"

Epilogue

SADLY, the tragedy of the Africans being exploited, trafficked and horribly abused in Hispaniola and specifically Saint-Domingue (now Haiti) was very real and is a matter of documented historical fact. Historical records are likely under-stated and nowhere near the reality of what actually took place. How can history record the excruciating pain, suffering, separation, loss, grief, fear, terror and horror the Africans endured? We can record the acts of violence, but how do we capture their individual emotions of fear, loss and pain? It, quite simply, cannot be done.

The African history in Haiti continued dramatically beyond the ending of this novel. Runaway slaves had banded together in the mountains and began their raids on the French plantations. Their numbers increased throughout the 18th century and they became an integral part of small revolutions against the French in 1791. They grew steadily from 1793 until 1804 as more and more slaves found freedom. In 1804 the African slaves overpowered their masters in a gigantic coup d'état. The 500,000 slaves on Saint-Domingue slaughtered the 35,000 French and the slaves became free and independent of French rule. It was the first time in recorded history that slaves successfully overthrew their captors.

After the takeover, the French government imposed a fine upon the new country of Haiti that was the equivalent of $21 billion in today's dollars. The debt was finally paid off in 1947. We can only imagine what would have happened if those funds had been kept in Haiti for the furtherance of their infrastructure, education and business development.

One of the cultural practices of modern-day Haiti is the restavek system. 300,000 children have been displaced from their birth families, due to poverty, to live with more well-to-do families as domestic servants. While a few of the children move to a better and more productive life, most have become essentially child-slaves.

The question asked by many is simple. How can a people whose history was all about being exploited, trafficked, abused and enslaved utilize the same methodology on their own country's children? How soon do we as people forget the tragedies of our own history?

The history of Haiti is one of heartbreak and tragedy. Many things are improving, but the present day reality is still about a country desperately trying to scratch and claw its way into survival and a better life.

The Haitian people will survive because they are among the most beautiful and resilient people on earth.